W9-BMX-591

# DEDICATION

**Matt Trammell:**
To Sarah, thank you for your unyielding love and constant encouragement. I love you more each day, Matt

**Marc Steren:**
To my parents, who always taught me to never give up on your dreams and to live every day with a smile- thank you and I love you, Marc

To Salome Mikadze, our outstanding research assistant, for her tremendous contributions to this book. From research to insight, your collaboration was invaluable. Thank you.

# TABLE OF CONTENTS

# INTRODUCTION: WHAT IS SCHOOL CULTURE FIT?

*"As a leader, you get the culture you create, and the nature of the culture affects what you can or cannot do in your organization."*
*- John Maxwell, January 21, 2020*

A teacher from another school came into my office, frustrated and uncertain about her future. Unchallenged in her current duties, she wanted more. After a few weeks of coaching, we had a plan in place. She would approach her supervisor with a layered proposal, requesting to take on more duties, work she was passionate about. This was going to be done without any discussion of money. Our thought was after a few months, the supervisor would see her value and give her a raise but at the very least, she would be engaged in a job she loved. Doing work that connected with her skillset and provided opportunity for growth.

The supervisor said he would get back to her. A week passed and no word. Two weeks, nothing. The third week she was back in my office and we polished off her resume, conducted a few mock interviews and sent her resume to schools where we thought her skills fit the position and the job description excited her. Two weeks later, she had accepted an exciting position at another school. Her current supervisor was shocked that she wanted to leave and asked if she would stay.

It was too late.

Tackling culture in any organization is a tremendous undertaking. Now try tackling culture in a school, with its numerous stakeholders: parents, students, alumni, faculty, and staff with little incentive to change, and you have a real challenge. In this book, we synthesize content from business, leadership, organizational behavior, industrial organizational psychology, educational pedagogy, and our own experiences to develop your "school's culture fit". School culture fit is the alignment of the school's major stakeholders under one clear purpose.

We have developed two frameworks to develop school culture fit, break through bureaucracies and promote growth. Our first framework enables stakeholders to discover your school culture fit, and the second describes how to ensure that the school culture fit endures. This book will guide you through first, adopting the frameworks to achieve the pre-determined traits of the school culture fit, while the second will ensure the fit persists. This will allow school stakeholders to:

    a.  engage in the process of discovering their school culture fit and

    b.  ensure it's continuous health.

## Section I: The Discovery Framework

The Discovery Framework emphasizes the importance of finding the stakeholders' jobs-to-be-done to formulate a school's true purpose. The framework provides tools to design tailored systems and processes to analyze and measure the outcomes of the school's purpose and to develop a "school culture fit" for all of the school's stakeholders.

*Discovery framework: jobs-to-be-done - school's purpose - systems and processes - measured outcomes*

## Section II: The 5 Stakeholders

In Section 2, we outline and discuss the five stakeholder groups comprising school culture, where each stakeholder group represents an important constituency for both private and independent schools.

School culture fit enables schools to align school stakeholders under a clearly defined purpose by matching student and faculty experiences with parent expectations. School leaders are then accountable for ensuring that the stimulating environment is consistently present, embracing the unified and inclusive culture that binds stakeholders together.

We examine closely the student experience, staff experience, parent expectations, school ecosystem, and school leaders' accountability.

# Section III: Continuous Evaluation

Once a school's culture fit is established and the frameworks have been fully utilized, leaders should work on maintaining the success. Sustainability is vital. Thus, we have developed a continuous evaluation framework to ensure school culture fit endures. The continuous evaluation framework incorporates the "flywheel" (Collins, 2001 & 2019). The flywheel describes how driving a new strategy is like getting a huge flywheel into motion. Initially, there is no movement. Yet with great exertion of will, the school is able to deliver small results that get the flywheel moving. Initial progress may appear minimal and trivial, but create the credibility to achieve more ambitious results. As results accumulate, more and more people throw their weight behind the wheel and the momentum of the flywheel builds and builds. Our flywheel of continuous evaluation is outlined below:

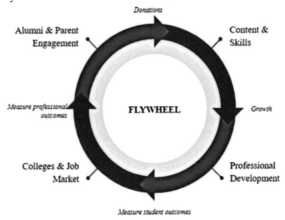

*Continuous Evaluation: (flywheel) content & skills - growth - professional development - measure student outcomes - colleges and job market - measure professional outcomes - alumni and parent engagement - donations of time and money*

# Section IV: 12 Foundational Cultural Traits

Next, we discuss twelve foundational, cultural traits needed to support a thriving school culture fit. These cultural traits fuel the framework described above and speak to the soul of school culture fit. For a school leader, these traits must be present not only to achieve school culture fit, but to preserve it as well.

# Section I: The Discovery Framework

*"We all have many jobs-to-be-done in our lives. Some are little; some are big. Some surface unpredictably; some regularly. When we buy a product, we essentially "hire" it to help us do a job. If it does the job well, the next time we're confronted with the same job, we tend to hire that product again. And if it does a crummy job, we "fire" it and look for an alternative."*
*(Christensen, 2016)*

## Section 90-92

On a warm Friday night, my family joined some dear friends from Tennessee. We met up in Baltimore, Maryland for the Orioles game. It was a wonderful evening filled with a sense of togetherness.

The thunderstorm, looming over the city before the first pitch, moved in another direction. The skies cleared. We enjoyed watching the kids delight in the atmosphere of Camden Yards. They were enthralled with the sights, sounds, smells, and of course, those mythical heroes on the field who move gracefully and powerfully as they do their work.

As adults, we revelled in overdue conversations. Catching up on life's events over the previous years took a couple of innings. The remainder of the game seemed just like old times - like we had never been apart. And hey, the Orioles won, so that doesn't hurt.

Still, one of the most amazing aspects of the evening was our section usher, Warren. We expected he would help us to our seats and perhaps be available to answer questions, should we have any. But, Warren did so much more.

He was as responsible for the incredible evening our families enjoyed as the game itself. Simply put, he made us feel like we were the most important people in the stadium.

Warren really loves his job as an usher in Section 90–92 at Camden Yards. It is evident in the genuine joy emanating from him, inning by inning. For Warren, however, joy did not reside in a title-but rather in the experience that he was able to create for the people sitting in his section.

Throughout the game Section 90–92 was buzzing. Warren literally never stopped moving. I am confident our families were not the only fans who enjoyed every moment of the game. His entire attention was devoted to the fans in his section. Warren was fully present. He brought his whole self to the job.

Yet he also took tremendous pride in the Orioles organization. No one cheered louder than him when an Oriole made a great play. Warren's pride in his own work and performance, combined with that in serving as a member of the Orioles organization, fuels his impeccable service to his fans.

Warren was aligned with the interests of the fans and that of the organization. He displayed a caring, passion-filled approach to honoring the opportunity his job provides. Nothing in Section 90–92 was out of place. No one was uncomfortable. Need a recommendation for which vendor in the park has the best hot dog? Warren is ready to provide it. Curious as to how the Orioles have been playing over the past few games? Warren is happy to share a cogent update. No one sits alone or feels left out in Section 90–92. You are a part of his community, and in this 'neighborhood' we all have fun together. It's no accident that this section started a long-lasting crowd 'wave' somewhere in the 8th inning.

In every customer experience, opportunities exist for peak moments to occur and lasting memories to be made. My family enjoyed a peak moment of our own midway through the game.

Between innings, the big league players throw the ball around to stay loose. As the 2-minute interim period between innings comes to a close, players sometimes toss the ball into the stands as a souvenir for a lucky fan. Warren saw this as an opportunity to provide a peak experience for a fan in Section 90–92.

Between innings Warren was standing with our kids, jumping up and down, while screaming for the center fielder to throw the ball to the kids in his section. My son now has a big-league ball - the peak moment for him, and the peak moment for me.

Warren created several peak moments for the fans in Section 90–92. When I book my next family trip to Camden Yards, I already know which section I will be sitting in. And I may just come back sooner than I had previously planned.

There is no doubt in my mind that Warren's approach to his work has a significant impact on the bottom line of the Orioles organization. Because of his unique approach and passion, how many other fans have returned sooner than they otherwise would have? How many lifelong Orioles fans has he developed by creating these peak moments? How many fans have left a game, and as a result of sitting in Section 90–92, went and told their friends about the amazing experience they enjoyed at Camden Yards?

Warren's example also adds tangible value for school leaders and those aspiring to school leadership roles. Warren understood the job to be done for the family- to have a wonderful experience at the ballpark. The Orioles and Warren also understood that in order to satisfy the job to be done, they needed to be aligned, from the vendors in the stands to the ballplayers down on the field. Together, they needed a "culture fit" to fulfil the family's job to be done. The win, which was nice, was merely a bonus.

What if a school's leadership team took this approach to their work every day? What if they established a school culture where this type of excellence, commitment to others, and joy, was the norm and expectation for all team members? How many personnel conflicts would be avoided because team members were aligned in school culture fit to deliver on the families' job to be done? And with all the energy and talents of the staff aligned towards this end, how much better would the school serve students and families?

The truth of the matter is this: all the policy and staff training in the world are worth very little if they omit a genuine commitment to service on the part of all team members. If teams are to win, all the players have to care. And they have to be committed to giving of themselves even when it may not be easy, comfortable, or convenient.

When both instructional and non-instructional staff members

display this level of commitment, schools indeed win. When schools win, students are transformed into the best versions of themselves. This is what a winning school culture looks like.

It all starts with leadership, of course. School leaders must model the proper way to do it, which certainly requires the passion of Warren.

This story illustrates the promise of empowering individuals through proactively managing the culture of the organization. Schools should empower teachers and other stakeholders, within a systematic framework, to develop a winning culture. School culture fit is essential for establishing this environment that generates maximum, positive impact. To successfully approach this first stage, we prioritize efforts on implementing the "Discovery Framework".

The Discovery Framework is a linear process with four sections that are dependent upon the preceding level: Jobs-to-be-done→School's Purpose→Systems and Processes→Measured Outcomes. By understanding what each of your stakeholders are trying to accomplish at each step, your school will be able to better focus your resources on the goals to be accomplished.

# JOBS-TO-BE-DONE (JTBD)

As a department chair, I sometimes oversee meetings between concerned parents and teachers in my department. In one such meeting, a father was upset about his son's grade. The teacher was patiently explaining that his son was struggling with a few concepts. I approached the meeting with a focus as to how we could help his son understand the concepts better in the future. After listening to the dad, it became apparent that he was less concerned with his son understanding the concepts as opposed to receiving a better grade so his son would stand a better chance to attend the college of his choice. Conversely, the teacher was less concerned about his grade and more that the student would understand the concept for future use.

Once I understood what each party wanted to achieve, I could fashion a solution for each. We provided the son with extra credit opportunities, thus satisfying the dad's desire to see a better grade and he would only be granted the extra credit if on those extra credit opportunities, he demonstrated mastery over the materials, thus satisfying the teacher's need that the son understand the concepts.

Jobs-to-be-done is a business approach to developing products based on understanding both the customer's "job to be done" and the thought processes that would lead that customer to "hire" the product to complete the job. When using this framework, a product team attempts to discover what its users are actually trying to accomplish or achieve when they buy a product or service (Christensen, 2016).

As entrepreneur and author Guerric de Ternay explains, product managers can use the jobs-to-be-done framework in two ways:

1. To get a better understanding of what their target market wants or needs;
2. To create a compelling customer experience.

In applying jobs-to-be-done theory to schools, school leaders should aim to understand what parents are *"trying to achieve"* for their children and ascertain why parents would *"hire"* the school (Christensen, 2016). The answer(s) to this question drives the school's purpose, internal processes and systems, while also informing how to measure outcomes.

Too often, schools form committees to address issues, create new programs, establish new strategies, or implement various forms of innovation without a thorough understanding of what their current and prospective families want to achieve. Failing to study consumer demand first, inevitably leads schools towards wasted resources and unsatisfied parents.

There is a clear, causal relationship between customer's jobs-to-be-done and customer satisfaction. The business principle that "a company can dramatically increase its chances for success at innovation if it knows precisely what metrics customers use to measure success and value when getting a job done" (Ulwick 2016) can be applied to schools.

The application for private and independent schools is direct. In order to achieve sustainable viability in the marketplace, schools must consistently meet and exceed the jobs-to-be-done of their families. Further, private and independent schools must deeply understand what their parents are *trying to achieve* by sending their children to their school and deliver overwhelming value to those j*obs-to-be-done ("JTBD")*.

Organizational behavior utilizes many diagnostic tools for discerning the jobs-to-be-done and we will use two of these tools to discover the jobs-to-be-done for schools: 1) empathetic interviews; 2) statistical surveys.

This triangulation of qualitative and quantitative data enables schools to make an informed decision as "the more information and the more ways the analyst can collect that information, the better the understanding of the job (Conte & Landy, 2007 p. 176). For jobs-to-be-done, we will:

a) Identify what the family wants to achieve through empathy interviews;

b) Discover how they are solving it now (alternative schools);

c) Analyze these existing alternative options through

statistical analysis and discern what component of the job is important but is not being solved well by the existing alternative;

d) Complete the JTBD journey for every stage and contrast it with their actual customer journey.

# EMPATHETIC INTERVIEWS

I coach many student startup teams. One such team, "Enleve" had the idea of placing a small, clear adhesive on the forearm so when the user tested different types of makeup, she wouldn't get smudges all over her skin. Before they entered into production of their product, the team went to Sephora to interview customers about their product. They wanted to understand the needs of their potential customers and there is no better way to achieve this than conducting empathy interviews.

After conducting over seventy interviews and truly listening to their customers, the Enleve team quickly realized that customers were happy with simply placing makeup on their skin and were not ready to *fire it*. Interestingly enough, a few customers had recently been painting their house and were frustrated that they had to keep painting over multiple test paints on their wall. With this insight, their new company was born, a company that provides clear adhesive to homeowners so they can test different types of paints without smearing the wall with each test application.

Empathy interviews are indispensable when trying to gather insights that otherwise might not be apparent.[1] This methodology uses a human-centered approach to understand the feelings and experiences of others. The flow of an empathy interview should feel less like an interview, and more like an open conversation. The goal is to understand your interviewees - to hear them, feel their emotion, and connect with the experiences they share.

Empathy interviews are step one for school leaders. During an empathy interview, school leaders can observe the interviewee's reaction, body language, their excitement or

---

[1] Blank, S., & Dorf, B. (2013). The Startup Owners Manual: The Step-by-Step Guide for Building a Great Company. Pescadero, CA: K & S Ranch Publ.

frustration, as well as hear their tone of voice. By asking open-ended questions and doing far more listening than talking, leaders learn valuable insights from real stakeholders to take back to the team for a truly informed session.

The interview process is designed for inquiry only, and should not turn into a promotional activity to "sell" the school. It takes patience and discipline to conduct jobs-to-be-done interviews. One common mistake that interviewers make is rushing to list all the benefits and resources the school has to offer. However, the secret of these interviews is to *listen* to the family's needs and what the family is trying to achieve. Active listening and non-suggestive questions allows school leaders to stay focused on the family and not the school, while gaining first-hand insights into the market segment.

The best way to identify how to differentiate your school from the competition is by talking to the families at competitor's or former schools. Their current pain points or significant gains are the single most important piece of information for your strategic planning.

Consider the following questions, amongst many tailored to your situations, when you are interviewing families:

1. What families hope to achieve at their current school and how do their expectations factor in their satisfaction?
2. Have their goals for their child changed and why are they considering switching?

Obtaining information about past decisions is extremely valuable since you can learn about families' motivations and expectations without directly asking them questions. 'Current School' JTBD also gives a better sense of where your school is positioned against the competition in the marketplace and how your brand offering could be differentiated for prospective families.

The interview process, in addition to discovering the jobs-to-be-done, allows schools to gather the following information:

a) Other schools have the family considered;

b) The price they have paid for schools in the past;
c) Their jobs-to-be-done at the current schools;
d) And the general fears and anxieties the family is experiencing and which of these are directly pushing them to consider a move to your school (Maurya, 2012).

# What schools are the family Considering "Consideration set"

Refers to the schools that interviewees have considered for their child(ren) in the past. This information will give the school a better sense as to who your school is really competing against and how to differentiate among the competition.

# Price the families are currently paying for school

How much have they paid in the past for school tuition? Though this information can be gleaned through market data, by gathering it directly from the family, the school can gauge the family's comfort level with past school expenditures. If this feels uncomfortable, a quick internet search of the current school's website provides quick access to this information.

# Jobs-to-be-done at the current school

What did the students and parents want to achieve at their prior school? Did they want to become better math students or learn how to socialize better with their classmates. By understanding what the stakeholders actually desired from their old school, it can help formulate their jobs-to-be-done at the new school.

# Anxiety and fears of the current school - can this lead to a switch to your school?

Aims to identify fears that families have from both their

current school and for the possibility of changing schools. Alleviating anxiety can become a strong force in motivating brand loyalty and building trust among the customers. For example, Uber, a ride-hailing mobile application, tells the user exactly when the Uber will arrive, the estimated time of arrival, the model of the car, and information on the driver.

This transparency inevitably alleviates the worry of when the Uber may arrive, unlike taxis, and eliminates the hustle in identifying the car and the driver. Schools should operate in a similar manner. Being aware of certain anxieties that parents are trying to avoid, and actively alleviating them, differentiates your school among others and forms a strong initial bond with families.

Through empathetic interviews, school leaders obtain a broader sense of each family's goals. However, the interview should not be limited to parents. School leaders should consider acquiring feedback from all the stakeholders involved with the school, such as the alumni, faculty, and students. An in-depth analysis of these responses will allow the alignment process of a shared culture to begin.

## Statistical Surveys

The next step is to *segment* what the stakeholders want to achieve into opportunities and levels of importance within the context of competing schools. The founder of innovation consulting firm Strategyn, Tony Ulwick utilizes a statistical approach to jobs-to-be-done (Ulwick, 2008). In conducting a competitive analysis, school leaders can utilize a partial application of Ulwick's statistical approach to discover two factors:

Out of the various competitors' *solutions,* which are the most *important* to the stakeholders?

Out of what is *important* to the stakeholder, what is *not* being solved well?

*Powerbee* was a student startup team that had developed a mobile phone charger that could fit in your pocket. The initial set of interviews revealed that their first customers were business travelers who struggled to find charging services at the airport.

So they conducted a statistical survey to see if it was important for them to have phone charging at the airport, or it was merely an inconvenience, and to see if they were satisfied with the way the airport currently solved that job to be done. A sample of this survey is below:

| How important is having your phone charged at the airport? | | | | |
|---|---|---|---|---|
| | Not important | Slightly important | Important | Very important |
| Row 1 | | | | |
| Row 2 | | | | |
| Row 3 | | | | |
| Row 4 | | | | |
| Row 5 | | | | |

| How satisfied are you with bringing your own charger? | | | | |
|---|---|---|---|---|
| | Not Satisfied | Slightly Satisfied | Satisfied | Very Satisfied |
| Row 1 | | | | |
| Row 2 | | | | |
| Row 3 | | | | |
| Row 4 | | | | |
| Row 5 | | | | |

A statistical survey is any structured inquiry designed to obtain aggregated data, which may be qualitative or quantitative where the individual or corporate identities of the respondents are in themselves of little significance. Statistical surveys in scope are not limited to those conducted by statistics divisions and do not necessarily involve completion of a form; telephone and personal interview surveys are also included (UNECE, 2000).

In conducting statistical surveys, there are a few things to keep in mind. A statistical survey is an investigation about the characteristics of a given population by means of collecting data from a sample of that population and estimating their characteristics through the systematic use of statistical methodology.

Stages of implementing the statistical survey are as follows:
- Planning the statistical survey.
- Formulating the goals and objectives of the statistical survey.
- Selecting survey sampling frame and statistical unit.
- Identifying the appropriate sampling design.
- Designing survey form.
- Collecting statistical data.
- Data processing and imputation for missing values.
- Statistical estimation.
- Data analysis.
- Disseminating data.

Let's summarize the steps we have discussed above:
1. Identify what the family wants to achieve through empathy interviews;
2. Discover how they are solving it now (alternative schools);
3. Analyze these existing alternative options through statistical analysis and discern what component of the job is important but is not being solved well by the existing alternative;
4. Complete the JTBD journey for every stage, which we discuss in more detail below, and contrast it with their actual customer journey.

From this information, we move to the next stage in the Discovery Framework - the school's purpose. A strong school purpose has the following elements:
a. Focused and concise statement;
b. Difference that matters to the stakeholder;

c.  Better solution for family's goals *(jobs-to-be-done).*

| Interviewer | Interviewee response: Parent/Student/Alumni/Faculty |
|---|---|
| What schools have you attended in the past? How about your siblings? | |
| Tell me about a formative time and experience at that school? | |
| What was missing at your past school? | |
| Why are you considering switching schools? | |
| What would you improve from your past school? | |
| How can our offerings be differentiated at our school? | |
| How did you hear about our school? | |
| What will you most miss about your past school? | |
| What are you most hoping to find in your next school? | |

# JTBD V. ACTUAL CUSTOMER EXPERIENCE/JOURNEY

The JTBD journey for students and their families is a very different experience from their actual "customer journey" (Meroni & Sangiorgi, 2011). The JTBD experience is what the students and family are *trying to achieve*. The customer journey for students and their families tracks their *actual* experience from the

| Stage | Description | Jobs-to-be-done | Actual experience |
|---|---|---|---|
| Admission stage | The information and gathering stage, such as campus visits and interviews with school leaders, teachers, current students. | | |
| Enrollment Stage | The preparation stage for school, obtaining course materials, class schedules. | | |
| School Day | The execution day- what the school day should look like, finding classes. | | |
| Social Integration Stage | Seeking out friends, fitting in and finding your right peer group. | | |
| Achievement Stage | Academic, athletic and social goals met. | | |
| Adjustment Stage | What social and academic adjustments do the students and family need to make? | | |
| Graduation Stage | Graduation from the division. | | |

admissions process through graduation, an actual "walk in their shoes" (Holmlid & Evenson, 2008). By analyzing empathetic interviews with data derived from statistical surveys, we can compare and identify the gap between what families are trying to achieve and actual experiences. The two journeys can be broken into stages and that will provide quantifiable insights that can easily translate into action plans for implementing the changes.

Listed below are the stages of the students' journeys.

# School's Purpose

*Marc's Story*

I was a bit of a mischievous child growing up and was told that if I misbehaved one more time, I was headed to private school. Not just any private school, but an all boys school that had a reputation as a pre-naval school. Of course, I slipped up and before I knew it, I was off to this private school.

I was in fifth grade and the experience was a bit unsettling. When teachers walked into the room you stood up and said, "Sir, yes sir." There were demerits and washing buses on Saturday morning was the norm. It was a change for sure. But it was a change for good.

Today, that very same school has changed dramatically. They started to accept girls. The disciplinary measure that the school was known for, simply went away to make room for a more modern approach. Graduating students were more likely to attend a prestigious private college then they were a military school.

This shift of the school's purpose may have been appropriate to the market, but was it done with the school's stakeholder's needs in mind? Or was it done to increase enrollment? Were my parents aware of this shift of the school's purpose? Were alumni and current families consulted about the change? How was change to the school's purpose derived? Our approach to school culture fit provides the groundwork for making informed decisions on what your school's purpose should be and how to ensure that everyone is aligned in that purpose.

Previous empathetic interviews and statistical data allow school leaders to obtain preliminary, actionable insight into the stakeholders' *jobs-to-be-done*. The next step is to gain absolute clarity on the school's purpose. A school's purpose should address the *jobs-to-be-done* by all of the stakeholders, with a focus on the priorities and points of difference that makes your brand stand out among the competition.

The purpose of an organization is of utmost importance. Still, most organizations struggle to accurately identify it. In a Harvard Business Executive Education class, Harvard professor Cynthia Montgomery challenges her students, who are high flying executives, to ask: "Why does your organization exist?" According to Montgomery: "Our [organization's] purpose is who we are and what makes us distinctive. It's what we as a company exist to achieve" (Montgomery, 2012).

High-performing and successful schools have a clear understanding of their purpose, allowing them to streamline the priorities of the school's leadership. The purpose is aligned with the expectations of all stakeholders and diligently communicated across the different levels of the institutions.

Empowered with information on what the stakeholders want to achieve and how competitors are perceived by the stakeholders, schools can find their unique purpose. In communicating your school's purpose, you should aim to communicate your purpose in 1-3 words. Such forced brevity will facilitate critical thinking and result in an acute identification of your core reason for existence.

Many thought leaders suggest individuals identify themselves by just one word (Carmichael, 2016). American author and speaker on leadership, Jon Gordon, adopts a similar practice of identifying one word to serve as a focus lead for each New Year. The one word guides an individual throughout the year and maintains efforts around priorities.

Gordon's strategy instructs on *how to act* during challenging moments and can be adopted for schools (Gordon, 2014). For schools, with so many stakeholders, we have borrowed the *one word* approach, expanding the limit to three words. For example, our school's motto is *caring, challenging, community*. In effect, those three words encapsulate our school's purpose: to provide our students with an exceptional education in a *caring and challenging community*.

These three words direct our school's policy, inform decisions and governance, and empower all staff to make decisions in alignment with our collective purpose. When facing difficult choices, teachers are able to ask themselves, "Am I being caring, have I challenged the student, and are my actions in the best interests of the community?"

Moreover, Adam Grant, a professor at the Wharton School and perhaps the world's leading researcher on giving, found that a school's purpose which resonates with alumni and parent stakeholders will generate larger donations (Grant, 2010). Aligning purpose with those who, at first sight may seem to have less of an immediate connection to the school, is integral for the long-term school culture fit. Parents and alumni serve as a bridge to the real world and by connecting with the school's purpose, every member of the community will enjoy the potential for life-long benefits, extending well beyond the secondary school years.

Ultimately, school leaders must adopt a long-term view when considering purpose. Such a view considers the entire school community to be a team. And the team's shared purpose allows it to collectively achieve more for one another than could possibly be achieved through individual endeavors. In his best-selling book, 11 Rings: The Soul of Success, legendary basketball coach Phil Jackson discussed the five stages of a team's development:

Stage 1: Team members believe life is full of despair, is futile, and thus operate from a dog-eat-dog worldview. Teamwork is temporary and transactional at best.

Stage 2: Team members are apathetic, have a hopeless outlook on their work, and thus just look to get by in their roles. Here, there is no vision.

Stage 3: Team members want to achieve. Yet they are out for

themselves. Individuals seek personal achievement above all else. Ambition is prevalent, yet it is deployed in a selfish and often, antagonistic manner.

Stage 4: Team members have a strong, collective identity grounded in being better than the competition. Their energy comes from dominating the competition and gaining superiority in the marketplace.

Stage 5: This is rarefied air, and occurs when team members have an innocent belief in, and conviction for, the possible. They are welded together in the collective belief that they have no limits as a unit and are committed to a goal bigger than each of their own, individual interests (2013).

It is this culminating, fifth stage that school leaders must seek and connect with their school's purpose. Here, all stakeholders are mutually committed to a purpose beyond their own interests. Abundance and joy underpin daring and invigorating work. When school communities achieve this level of purpose, school culture fit is achieved and sustaining.

# SYSTEMS AND PROCESSES

*Matt's story*

By nature, I like to operate by 'feel'. Consider my Myers-Briggs profile. I am an 'I' (introvert), 'N' (intuitive), 'F' (feeling), 'P' (perceiving). Interestingly, it has taken me about 15 years of reflection and work experience to understand who I truly am in this sense. As a 24 year old, I completed a Myers-Briggs Type Indicator and obtained a far different result. The truth is, the results I obtained at that time were aspirational. They reflected what I thought I wanted to be. What I thought I should be. Perhaps more directly, what I thought great leaders were. The INFP designation speaks to who I truly am; this result is informed with a strong self-knowledge.

While no designation is definitively accurate, the Myers-Briggs serves as a strong starting point. As an INFP, adhering to systems and processes can at times feel antithetical to my personality type. Often, I would prefer to 'feel' my way through a project or situation, leaning on my intuition, emotional intelligence, and general relational instincts.

Still, I understand the virtues of systems and processes and recognize the critical role they play in organizational success. Over the previous four years, I have stepped into two different leadership roles. As I stepped into the Assistant Principal role, I found systems and processes to be an indispensable tool. For example, every spring I was tasked with leading our Middle School's academic planning initiative for the upcoming school year. This was a critically important project to students, parents, teachers, and fellow school leaders. It included determining the number of sections each subject-area and grade-level would need, where teachers in each grade level would be placed, introducing and completing current student course selection, new student placement testing, and new student course selection.

The process stretched over several months.

My first year leading this effort was an experience, to say the least. While the process ended well, there was no shortage of angst and frustration on my part - at least behind the scenes. I relied too much on 'feel' and did not implement sufficient systems and processes.

I learned from that first year, and going forward I implemented a detailed table of dates, list of stakeholders, priorities, communication needs, tasks, progress updates, and notes for the upcoming school year. I adopted a systematic and process-based approach for this critically important task. I did not abandon my natural strengths, but instead complimented them with systems and processes.

As a result, I was more efficient. Stakeholders received more comprehensive, clear, and cogent emails. We stayed on schedule. And perhaps most importantly, my mental energy was freed from the cognitive load accompanying the burden of trying to keep all of these logistical pieces in my head. I moved these items from my head, and into a comprehensive, systematic process.

I also discovered that adopting a systematic process reduced tensions and conflicts. For example, as an INFP I am quite sensitive to the experience and mood of others. During my first year leading our Middle School's academic planning initiative, there were days where I delayed scheduling a meeting or 'adding something to a colleague's plate' because I knew how much they had going on. While this sensitivity is a virtue and can be appropriately deployed in many situations, a project such as this required an adherence to timelines and thus, deadlines. Systems and processes were needed.

During my second year, I could simply blame the timeline when tempted to allow my 'feeling' or 'perceiving' to interrupt necessary progress. A conversation could go something like this, "I know you have a lot going on this week, yet if we do not complete this meeting, we will fall behind on our timeline and the negative results will be $x$ and $y$." Implementing a systematic process to our Middle School's academic planning initiative allowed me to limit the downside of my personality type by providing the objective necessity to timely completion of a task. In year two and beyond, the entire project became a more enjoyable experience with better outcomes.

Systems and processes are critical tools for individuals and organizations alike. They serve to align actions to purpose, create efficiencies, and produce predictable outcomes. And they are critical tools as school's pursue school culture fit. A school's systems and processes contain three important elements:

1. Reward desired behaviors,
2. Create sustainable organizations,
3. Solves constraints.

Below, we go further into defining the elements of a strong system and how they apply to your operational activities.

## Reward Desired Behaviors

Organizations that implement a system that rewards desired behaviors, even small behaviors, can see a 15% increase in productivity (Boyle, 1987). Moreover, rewarding desired behaviors leads to better outcomes (Herzberg et al., 1959). School leaders must identify the organizational behaviors which align with their school's purpose and then create a system of formal incentives and rewards to reinforce them. Importantly, the incentives should not be limited to monetary rewards.

How does one reward a well-accomplished teacher when there is no more room in the budget for a pay raise? Such a reward should include, but not be limited to, recognitions at staff meetings, positive acknowledgement in formal reviews, celebrations through school-wide emails, personal notes of affirmation and recognition, and other internal communications. The public recognition signals to the rest of the staff the type of excellence valued by the school and affirms the outstanding teacher within the school community.

Schools must also be weary of designing zero-sum reward systems. Stack ratings, where there is a top and bottom ranking, automatically signals to your staff that you could be ranked very low, even though you are an excellent employee. Such a model produces scarcity and fear. It can also lead to infighting and a lack of collegiality. Instead, recognize high achievers as the standard without unnecessarily "ranking" less accomplished colleagues. As the adage suggests, 'you get more of what you celebrate.'

## Sustainable organizations

Our Entrepreneurship Department started out with just one hire and as the Department grew, a Director of Entrepreneurship position opened up. The search included candidates from up and down the east coast as well as internal candidates. Eventually, the position went to an internal candidate, minimizing the learning curve. More importantly, the internal candidate, who had spent 6 years at the school, reaped the benefit of being an "insider". She knew the opportunities where the program could improve and felt ownership and pride of the Department's past accomplishments. For other members of the school, they observed real growth opportunities as available within the school. They could find encouragement as the school rewarded an employee who stayed committed to the organization, while demonstrating sustained excellence. For the school, the training of the employee paid off as she is a dedicated team member and has grown into a new role.

Regardless of the industry, organizations face employee churn. To minimize opportunity cost of the recruiting process, sustainable institutions invest in employee training to promote dedicated professionals once the growth opportunity arises (Conte & Landy, 2019). A regular or proactive job analysis practice can help the organization in creating a proper infrastructure by defining the tasks to be performed as well as the timelines for fulfilling them. More often than not, managers run into a common mistake of devaluing the importance of growth within an organization.

Daniel Pink, New York Times bestselling author, in his book *Drive* found that the potential for growth is the number one factor for employee satisfaction, even outweighing monetary compensation (Pink, 2009). Private and independent schools must take proactive actions to foster internal leadership across all departments. This becomes particularly acute in regions densely populated with competing schools. The more the institutional landscape is competitive within an hour-drive reach, the more critical the issue of employee turnover becomes for the school. Your top employees can simply transfer schools if a better opportunity arises elsewhere and given the location advantage, the probability of job change significantly increases. In response to this reality, school leaders must thoughtfully develop, and provide growth opportunities for talented team members, to facilitate sustainable performance for the school itself. Such action will ultimately result not only in long-term excellence, but also contribute to a sustainable school culture fit.

# Constraints

Customized systems and processes also allow leaders to identify hidden constraints the school faces. These often invisible bottlenecks can significantly impact the environment and overall efficiency of the school.

Constraints are placed within economic, social, and political dimensions. For example, under the political domain, the *No Child Left Behind Act*[2] has narrowed the focus of the curricula and academic achievement through promoting excessive reliance on high-stake assessments to judge performance of stakeholders. The economic dimension is primarily triggered by the lack of resources and financial pressures that limit a school's ability to support academic and extracurricular needs of their students.

An excellent example of a constraint, at the time of this writing, is how COVID-19 has impacted organizations across the world. With employees quarantined at their homes, effective leaders have started to use technologies such as Zoom or Google

---

[2] Job analysis information will be used to identify future staffing needs (Morgan & Smith, 1996) and enable teams to maximize their work process efficiencies (Sanchez, 1994). Organizations that regularly conduct job analysis possess a much better knowledge of their employees' strength and limitations, and can take timely corrective action to improve any deficiencies in their skills and job behavior (Clifford, 1994).

Meet at scale to establish digital communication and resume their work online.

In the independent and private school setting, COVID-19 has created tremendous financial pressures for schools as they establish budgets for the upcoming school year and seek to finalize enrollment. For example, independent and private schools often establish an annual budget for financial aid. This allocation is utilized for current and newly enrolled families to help make the school financially accessible. In the COVID-19 economy, the financial needs of current and newly enrolled families have increased to historic levels, while the financial aid budget allocation for many schools remains largely static. Even as some schools implement one-time increases in financial aid, such as a COVID-19 Relief Fund for current families, the increase is likely proportionately small relative to the school's overall financial aid budget. Thus, schools are experiencing an unexpected, and historic, financial constraint.

Schools that are able to identify constraints early on, can mitigate the harm or cut it out of the system entirely. In resolving constraints, schools should look to "identify 'bright spots'" (Heath C. & Heath D., 2010). These "bright spots" are solutions to constraints found in one part of the organization that can be modeled to solve a constraint in another part of the organization. By optimizing available tools and looking at the points of intersection, school leaders can more effectively allocate resources to address constraints. This does not mean schools will not face historic constraints such as COVID-19. Nonetheless, identifying "bright spots" and employing a creative problem-solving approach can position schools to emerge from challenging situations in a posture of strength and with their school culture fit intact.

# MEASURED OUTCOMES

Google has developed a measurement system known as OKRs, or Objectives and Key Results (Doerr, 2018). Teams at Google set "objectives" which are time-boxed goals. These objectives are chunked into smaller, "key results" that are continually measured to track progress. Such a system has many advantages in a school setting. In the timeboxing process model, each unit is assigned a time box. As a result, team members can efficiently allocate the time and accomplish more pre-determined goals (Jalote, at al. 2004).

As you are incorporating effective time management in order to maximize the efficiency of your operations, keep in mind that there are other factors that can ensure positive results when it comes to instilling a vibrant and productive school environment. First, departments should work together in order to jointly declare objectives. This collaborative effort empowers school faculty and confers ownership of the objectives. An individual result is now the collective achievement of the entire team. The culture of 'we' proves to be extraordinarily useful in any community, and especially practical in a school environment. Moreover, greater job control and autonomy leads to greater job satisfaction and reduces burnout (Conte & Landy, p. 405).

Second, even large organizations such as Google need to limit the number of objectives. In *The One Thing*, the author contemplates ways to declare and stay focused on his "most important thing" (Keller, 2012). Google's operational procedures force schools and - on a more micro level - departments, to stay focused on one or two of the most significant objectives that all stakeholders are willing to support. As Shawn Achor noted in *Big Potential,* employing a collaborative approach and staying convergent on goals enhances the experiences and makes everyone on the team more productive (Achor, 2018).

The third tactic accentuates the notion that key results are accomplished in smaller chunks. As a result of such an approach, the "chunked" results offer a crucial opportunity for a positive change. Chunking becomes a new method for the team to achieve more in a shorter period of time, which is not only efficient but self-rewarding as well. In addition, stakeholders can remain actively engaged since they can track progress in increments as opposed to seeing whether an objective was achieved or not in the end of the year only (Fogg, 2020). These smaller benchmarks ensure that the students remain on the correct pathways, making smaller pivots possible and avoiding the massive correction that may occur at the end of the course.

# SECTION 1 REFERENCE LIST

*Achor, S. (2018). Big potential. New York, NY: Crown Business.*

*Boyle, D . (1987, May) Harvard Business Review. The 100 Club Retrieved from http://web.a.ebscohost.com/ehost/pdfviewer/pdfviewer? vid=6&sid=76a9a594-f0cd-4ba8-b25f- 1530ad924942%40sessionmgr4006*

*Britton, D & Gordon, J & Page, J (2013) One Word That Will Change Your Life, Hoboken, NJ John Wiley & Sons*

*Carmichael, E. (2016). Your One Word. New York, NY Penguin.*

*Christensen, C. M. (2016). Competing against luck. New York, NY: HarperBusiness.*

*Conte, J & Landy, F (2019) Work in the 21st Century,6th Edition Hoboken, NJ John Wiley & Sons.*

*Coyle, D (2018) The Culture Code: The Secrets of Highly Successful Groups, New York, NY, Bantam Books*

*Doerr, J. (2018). Measure What Matters. New York: Portfolio/Penguin*

*Fogg, B. J. (2020). Tiny habits: the small changes that change everything. Boston: Houghton Mifflin Harcourt.*

*Gordon, J. (2014). The carpenter: a story about the greatest success strategies of all. Hoboken, NJ: Wiley.*

Grant, A (2010, February) Knowledge @Wharton Putting a face to a name; the Art of Motivating Employees, Retrieved from https://knowledge.wharton.upenn.edu/article/putting-a-face-to-a-name-the-art-of-motivating-employees/.

Gray, D. "Updated Empathy Map Canvas." Medium. 15 July 2017. https://medium.com/the-xplane-collection/updated-empathy-map-canvas-46df22df3c8a

Jackson, P. & Delehanty, H. (2013). 11 Rings: The Soul of Success. New York, NY: Penguin Press.

Jalote, Pankaj & Palit, Aveejeet & Kurien, Priya. (2004). "The Timeboxing Process Model for Iterative Software Development." Advances in Computers. 62. 67-103. 10.1016/S0065-2458(03)62002-4.

Heath, C. & Heath, D. (2010) Switch: How to Change Things When Change is Hard, New York, NY: Broadway Books.

Herzberg, F., Mausner, B., & Snyderman, B. (1959). The motivation to work (2nd ed.). New York: John Wiley.

Keller, G. W., & Papasan, J. (2012). The one thing. Austin, TX: Bard.

Maurya, A. (2012) Running Lean. Sebastopol, CA, O'Reilly.

Montgomery, C. (2012) The Strategist: Be the Leader Your Business Needs. New York: HarperCollins.

Pink, D. (2009). Drive: The surprising truth about what motivates us.New York, NY Riverhead Books.

Economic Commission for Europe of the United Nations (UNECE), (2000). "Terminology on Statistical Metadata", Conference of European Statisticians Statistical Standards and Studies, No. 53, Geneva.

*Yohn, D. L (2018), Fusion: How Integrating Brand and Culture Powers the World's Greatest Companies Boston, MA Nicholas Brealey Publishing.*

# Section 2: Five Stakeholders of School Culture Fit

*"Culture isn't just one aspect of the game - it is the game. In the end, an organization is nothing more than the collective capacity of its people to create value." - Lou Gerstner*

As we are venturing towards creating and sustaining a school culture fit, we should recognize the importance of managing all five key stakeholders comprising the school community. These stakeholders include your students, staff, parents, school ecosystem, and school leaders. Understanding how your school engages with each of these groups, while optimizing their experiences and contributions, is a critical step to achieving and maintaining school culture fit.

# STUDENT EXPERIENCE

## Student's Job to be Done

The student experience refers to the balance between academics, arts, athletics, community service, and emotional intelligence. It is critical that schools achieve high-level programming in each, while ensuring all five domains are addressed through dynamic and relevant curriculum designed individually for the school culture fit. In evaluating the student's experience, we revert back to looking at the jobs-to-be-done for students. What are students trying to achieve at your school?

For the many pressures that accompany the modern student, their jobs-to-be-done can be broken into three achievements (Osterwalder & Pugneur, 2010):

| | |
|---|---|
| **Functional jobs-to-be-done** | What are students trying to achieve from the school, such as earn good grades, graduate, and earn admission into a good college? |
| **Emotional jobs-to-be-done** | How should the school make the student feel internally - intrinsic qualities such as emotional intelligence, self awareness and confidence? |
| **Social jobs-to-be-done** | How do the students want to be perceived by others such as his/her peers, teachers, parents, colleges and eventual employers? |

The school must provide meaningful opportunities for all students in these areas and be able to achieve measurable growth. This is not a call for more testing, but instead a framework to gauge "progress" among students. Using the simple questions below, school leaders will be able to observe what information students retained and what mattered most to them, the degree to which students are prepared for new learning, and fluctuations

| What did I learn yesterday? | |
|---|---|
| What will I want to learn today? | |
| What subjects are interesting to me? | |

in subject-area student interest.

Perhaps most critical, schools must strive to create an emotionally safe and yet, invigorating, environment. Here, students compete internally vs. externally. Rather than competing against one another to earn the highest grade on a test for example, they compete against themselves, striving to achieve their best self and advance their performance. The goal is to move as close to one's potential as possible. This allows for a culture of excellence, wrapped in social and emotional support, to flourish.

First and foremost, the student experience revolves around the daily in-class and extracurricular activities students are engaged in while on campus. The student experience then expands to include their morning and evening routines. This "total curriculum" represents the stretch of time from the point students enter the bus or car in the morning and up to when they finish working on their homework in the evening hours.

The daily student journey is compared to insights learned during jobs-to-be-done interviews conducted earlier. Is the journey achieving the student's jobs-to-be-done? Knowing your school culture, desired student experience versus actual student experience, you can adjust the programming to focus on the most beneficial factors to increase student engagement, productivity, and satisfaction.

## Schedule

Effective schedules allow the school day to be strategically organized both for students and teachers. Timed activities enhance student experience and significantly increase their productivity.

In 1843, Horace Mann designed the classroom based on Prussian efficiency to teach our children to become better factory workers (American Academy of Arts and Sciences, 1873). The 19th century education model stemmed less from a belief in the economic or moral imperative of education for all children and more from a desire to simply create a tolerant, orderly, and civilized society.

Too often, even though there have been many technological

advancements, our collective educational approach remains largely the same. Children have a limited attention span during lectures, especially when the new material is taught in a dry and less than engaging manner (Rose, 2012). Content can be made interesting, and every effort to do so must be made.

It is also critical that soft skills be emphasized during teaching. Previous material should be summarized at the beginning of each class period, with strong connections clearly articulated to the new material that will be covered in the current class period. This creates a "curriculum bridge" for students and increases the likelihood of content acquisition.

In the most innovative classrooms, students are engaged, solve authentic problems, and acquire content knowledge while developing critical skills such as collaboration, communication, time management, project management, and problem-solving. Today's innovative classrooms are combining teacher-led instruction, student collaborative activities, software, virtual instructors, and a complex scheduling algorithm. Such an approach potentially allows each student to independently move through an individualized learning progression at their own pace.

Despite the instructional innovations described in many of today's most innovative classrooms, we believe there is another critical component to the student experience that has yet to be adequately addressed. In short, the traditional school-wide scheduling system is ineffective and flawed at its core. The scheduling of the high schools, in particular, indicates much of the issue.

For school leaders, it is never an easy task to schedule the day. Logistical constraints are nearly endless. And the workings of a school are intricately interdependent. Nonetheless, what follows is a suggestive model to begin the conversation at your school. From this outline, school leaders have the opportunity to adjust and mold specific applications in a way that best fits their school culture.

## The most difficult problem first

Roy Baumeister first presented the theory of ego depletion by noting that those who resisted chocolate in the morning "depleted" their willpower and made poorer decisions later in the day than those who opted to simply have a bite of chocolate (Baumeister, R. F., et. al, 1998). Although the theory of ego depletion has been debunked in many academic circles, there are a lot of benefits that come with teaching children how to address the most difficult problems first thing in the morning. In fact, in a study conducted by the Stanford psychologist Carol Dweck and her colleagues, published in Proceedings of the National Academy of Sciences, Dweck concluded that signs of ego depletion were observed only in test subjects who believed willpower was a limited resource. Those participants who did not see willpower as a finite resource did not show signs of ego depletion (Job et al., 2013).

And yet we see true benefits of tackling the most important thing in the first session of the day. In The ONE Thing: The Surprisingly Simple Truth Behind Extraordinary Results (Keller & Papasan, 2017), the authors urge us to ask ourselves: what's the ONE thing you can do, such that by doing it, everything else will be easier or unnecessary? It's about going small, and becoming laser-focused on what truly matters. In essence, students may dedicate their energy and willpower to solving the most complicated problems and their most challenging classes, deploying their strongest resources to meet their greatest need.

## Mid-morning break

If we look at many of the masters of productivity, for example, we see a specific pattern in how they constructed their day. They worked in the morning, conducting uninterrupted Deep Work and then rested their minds through a different activity (Newport, 2018). Deep Work allowed them to focus without distraction on a cognitively demanding task, quickly mastering complicated information and producing better results, in less time. Scenic walks, playing the guitar or some other form of physical activity were all means to discharge and get ready for the next working sprint. Regardless of the specific activity, each offered a clear break from their previous engagement and created space for restoration.

In Rest, the author provides another perspective on famous

masters, such as Hemingway and Degas (Pang, 2017). Alex Pang notes that they were able to collect their thoughts and let other parts of the brain work on the problem by engaging in these light forms of physical activity. While their conscious minds enjoyed "placebo" rest, their unconscious minds continued to work on the problem. This phenomenon is supported by research. Two examples include Learning How to learn (Coursera, 2018) and this Stanford study (Oppezzo, 2014) that found that we become more creative with a walk as opposed to sitting at our desks. Walking outside produces the most novel and highest quality results for Guilford's alternate (GAU) test of creative, divergent thinking and the compound remote associates (CRA) test of convergent thinking. Moreover, it was found that walking opens up the free flow of ideas, and it is a simple and robust solution to the goals of increasing creativity and physical activity.

The key is to shift our value perception of breaks. We are not suggesting the mid-morning break last for 30 minutes or longer. Likely, such a break would last for 15-20 minutes. During this time, students are still learning. Their minds are processing and filing content learned from the previous class period(s). Their batteries are recharging, thereby increasing the student's capacity for learning throughout the remainder of the day. And finally, space is created for creativity and reflection. The question school leader's must answer is not if a mid-morning break is appropriate, but instead, how can it be constructed to maximize these powerful cognitive benefits?

# Lunch

We have all heard the old adage, "you are what you eat." While this may not be up for literal application, the message rings true. What we eat matters. And what our students eat, most certainly matters.

It's unfortunate how we nourish our students, with high sugar and foods loaded in carbohydrates. Recent studies have demonstrated that nutrition affects students' thinking skills, behavior, and health, all factors that impact academic performance. Research further suggests that diets high in trans and saturated fats can negatively impact learning and memory. In addition, nutritional deficiencies early in life can affect the cognitive development of school-aged children. Furthermore, there is overwhelming evidence that access to nutrition improves students' cognition, concentration, and energy levels (Liu, at al. 2017). Disciplinary actions also have been shown to decrease in schools that offer a universal-free school breakfast program (Murphy, Drake, & Weineke, 2005; Wahlstrom & Begalle, 1991). And sadly, children who do not get sufficient meals are more likely to repeat a grade (Alaimo et al., 2001; Kleinman et al., 1998).

As suggested in the award-winning book on the mind and the body, *The Brain Warrior's Way*, our brain needs nutrition high in protein, rich in fibers and plant-based nutrients (Amen, 2017). If your school is truly committed to providing students with a world-class experience, you must align as many resources as possible to ensure they are provided with the proper nutrition while at school. Otherwise, we are expecting our students to perform without the fuel needed to bring their best selves to each class or activity. Improving the nutritional value of the food students eat in the dining hall, snack bar, and vending machines is a significant endeavor, one that will require a culture change and financial investment. It's worth it.


## The afternoon

The afternoon should be focused on more collaborative efforts and acquiring soft skills. Potential emphases during this time of the school day include public speaking, empathy, listening and leadership skills. Additional programming such as advisory, clubs, assemblies, and other enrichment opportunities are well-suited for the afternoon options as well.

Again, the idea is not to make the afternoons less important. School leaders should reinforce that the last few hours of the day are critical aspects of the overall curriculum. Designing the school day in this manner, to the degree logistically feasible, ensures students bring their full energy and will-power to their most challenging responsibilities first thing in the morning, while remaining productive throughout the afternoon.

A more comprehensive research comes from the field of

neuroscience. The right hemisphere is dominant in afternoon hours allowing for processing of visual information and long-term memory (Klein, 2001). Processing of visual and audiological stimuli, spatial manipulation, facial perception and artistic ability seem to be right hemisphere functions. When planning educational sessions in the afternoon, basic neuroscience should be taken into consideration.

## End of day

Ideally, in lieu of homework, students would reflect on the day's learning once they get home. Multiple studies suggest that we retain more of the content through reflection and learning. Moreover, we need to provide time for our diffused mind to rest and facilitate the creative process (Oakley, 2019).

Too often, students arrive home, after practice, dinner, and an additional commitment, only to shower and tackle hours of homework. Followed up with an early morning wake-up, and starting the same process all over again, it is not surprising that our students often feel overwhelmed and approach their classwork reluctantly as opposed to joyfully. Needless to say, such a pattern is accompanied by an unhealthy lack of sleep, establishing a routine that is far from the balanced life that promotes creativity and problem-solving.

Additionally, it is essential to emphasize a sense of community and family time. How can this be accomplished when our children are tied up in their rooms at all hours of the night completing homework?

## Content Acquisition and Retention

It is important to "space out" the learning and use different techniques of teaching. Students will retain more of the content if they have to stretch their minds and try to recall the content a few days after the lesson as opposed to daily rote learning. An excellent discussion of this topic can be found in the bestselling book, Make it Stick (Brown, 2018). Instructional variety, allowing students to access their knowledge and apply their developing skill sets in a fresh way, facilitates meaningful, enjoyable, and 'sticky' learning. In other words, different days, different problems.

Additionally, students benefit from solving authentic problems. This process allows students to engage with the content, create meaning, and then apply their learning to solve a real problem. In doing so, they combine deep content learning with skill development, expressed through a student-centered instructional design.

# Beyond Content Acquisition

Though content will play a significant role, schools must also provide the resources to enrich the curriculum and strengthen students in the following areas:

## *Soft Skills*

The term soft skills is likely one we have all heard and even used in conversation. Still, it can be a bit vague. Soft skills are associated with communication, collaboration, and problem solving. And in our digital and global workplace, soft skills have never been more valuable.

In the workplace, these skills are utilized everyday and schools need to make a concerted effort to make sure students develop them through the years. Soft skills can be classified into two categories: intrapersonal skills and interpersonal skills. Intrapersonal skills refer to an individual's ability to manage oneself for optimal performance. Skills such as time management, stress management and creative thinking. Meanwhile, interpersonal skills are defined as an individual's ability to manage their relationship with others for optimal work performance. Examples include the ability to empathize, motivate, to lead and to negotiate (Weiner, 2000).

## *Emotional Intelligence (EQ)*

As defined by Dr. Bradberry in *Emotional Intelligence,* self awareness is the ability to adapt cognitively, behaviorally, and emotionally to the moment (Bradberry, 2009). First, emotionally intelligent students may be able to deal more easily with negative emotions elicited by academic settings. The prototypical academic emotion is test anxiety, but there are a variety of other emotions specific to academic settings. For example, students need to regulate the disappointment of lower than-expected test scores or negative feedback, or the boredom involved in learning concepts and subject matter that are of instrumental rather than intrinsic interest (e.g., learning a tax code to pass an accountancy exam; Pekrun, et al., 2010).

Emotional intelligence also speaks to a student's ability to fluently navigate difficult conversations, 'read the room', sense the needs and moods of their peers, recognize non-verbal cues, and connect team members of differing opinions towards a common resolution. Such skills are in high demand in the workplace. And as such, school leaders must thoughtfully implement their development into the student experience.

## *Learning how to learn*

A leading professional in engineering, Barbara Oakley, from *Mindshift* discusses 'learning how to learn' as the new advantage of the life-long learner for career advancement and emotional health. Research has shown that the ability to use a variety of cognitive and metacognitive strategies is important to be successful in many types of learning and study tasks (Pintrich & De Groot, 1990; Pintrich & Garcia, 1991). The attention on 'learning to learn' is also stimulated by the policy in the Dutch speaking part of Belgium which imposed 'learning to learn' as one of the objectives for secondary schools. It is stated that schools and teachers have to spend time on 'learning to learn' throughout all the different subjects.

'Learning to learn' could be described as "a skill, or more plausibly as a package of skills, involving study skills, critical analysis, time management, planning, goal setting and so on" (Rawson, 2000, p. 225). It is the responsibility of school leaders to determine the scale of implementation within their schools. 'Learning to learn' could include study skills of a learner undertaking a fairly structured program or a skill set of a self-managed learner (Rawson, 2000). The difference between the 'isolated' and the 'embedded' way of implementing 'learning to learn' refers to the place where it is addressed: outside or inside regular courses.

For many researchers, the discussion about the implementation of 'learning to learn' ends with a plea for an embedded approach. On the other hand, we argue that the efficiency is more appropriately determined by the way 'learning to learn' is 'put into practice' than by the fact of whether it is organized outside or inside regular courses. The key is to ensure that students leave with the skills, knowledge, and self-awareness needed to become reflective learners throughout their lives.

## *Athletic metrics*

One critical component of the Progress Principle is to provide immediate feedback (Amabile & Kramer, 2011). In athletics, immediate feedback is a component of good coaching. It is also an integral aspect of improvement for athletes. As a former basketball player, I (Matt) fondly remember many of my coaches. They were mentors and prominent resources for my improvement. As a player, the feedback I most appreciated was provided in real time, short and to the point, and wrapped in positivity.

From there, the metric I was responsible for was daily, personal improvement. My coaches did not measure my performance relative to that of my teammates. Instead, my 'today' was simply measured against 'my yesterday'. Such an approach to improvement and growth is naturally differentiated. Each player is held to their own metric, and the skills that need developing become a focal area for training and practices. In this way, students are able to achieve daily wins in their athletic endeavors, while also being moved beyond their comfort zones. Indeed, stretching students beyond their comfort zones in a personalized manner will lead students to the intrinsic satisfaction that derives from accomplishment (Meer & Buijs, 2012, pp. 243-244).

# Artistic growth

By providing the right resources and by assessing progress, we can help students achieve true, measurable growth in the visual and performing arts. According to Eisner (2003), arts are an integral part of human affective experience. One reason proponents cite for integrating artistic skills with the overall academic program is the perception that works of art can engage the students at an emotional level, thereby enriching the curriculum, as well as their social/emotional experience (Eisner, 2003).

In fact, Eisner also identified four effects or findings from art education experience:

1.  Students learn the process of putting ideas and expressions into a form or creation.
2.  Students gain greater perceptual abilities and become more analytical.
3.  Students see interconnectedness between arts, culture, and history.
4.  Students demonstrate perseverance through ambiguity (Eisner, 2003).

Undoubtedly, artistic growth is a critical aspect of the student experience. The benefits of providing immediate feedback most certainly apply as students create and express themselves through projects. The art teacher, or classroom teacher, acts as a coach. They also serve as encouragers, advocates, and champions for their students. As students develop their artistic skills, as well as their creative and expressive abilities, teachers can support students through a focus on daily growth.

# STAFF EXPERIENCE

Instructional and non-instructional staff play an integral role in creating school culture fit. The staff experience refers to how a school's employees feel while at school and how connected they are to the organizational mission. Their experience can be substantially enhanced by proactively creating a collaborative and intellectually-challenging environment.

| | |
|---|---|
| *Functional jobs-to-be-done* | To be able to teach students to the best of your ability |
| *Emotional jobs-to-be-done* | To be able to produce work that is engaging, challenging, and that I can be proud of |
| *Social jobs-to-be-done* | To be recognized by the school for the value I bring to students, their families, and the entire school community. |

*Marc's Story*

A couple of years ago, I was working 100 hours a week. In addition, I had over 100 employees, which inevitably led to increased stress and anxiety levels. My business was failing and my family life was a disaster. My wife would arrange playdates for me with my own kids. How pathetic was that?

Of course, after 10 minutes of these play dates, I would receive a call from one of the stores and would be unable to decline, leaving my kids crying and wife disappointed, in my wake. Was that the turning point?

Maybe the turning point was the day my chest felt like there was an enormous elephant sitting on it. I rushed to the hospital, thinking I was having a heart attack. The doctor said it wasn't a heart attack, but rather stress and anxiety. More importantly, if I didn't get it under control, I would be dead in a few years.

I was in my mid 30s. Fortunately, together with my mentor, I found a way out. I learned that I could really have it all: business success, a happy family, and a meaningful life with a higher purpose.

The key, I discovered, was time management and recognizing signs of burnout. Now that I am a teacher myself, I want to share some of these life lessons of time management with you. Together, we can refine our everyday lives and those of your staff.

Staff members can only thrive in an environment that promotes both their personal and professional development. Your faculty members will then serve as an example for your students to learn and professionally grow. By nature and in purpose, schools are safe spaces designed for learning and growth. This is the explicit purpose for students of any educational institution.

The same ethos should also apply and pertain to your staff members.

Stated another way, the staff experience must be designed to "live" the school purpose. Learning and growth should be indispensable to the staff experience. Such a culture provides several benefits. First, staff develop a deeper connection and loyalty to the school as they view it as a source of their development. Second, students see their teachers learning, growing, and embracing a commitment to improvement. Such an example then promotes their own commitment to learning and growth. Finally, staff from other schools observe the growth and enthusiasm demonstrated by their peers and desire to work at the school as well.

It is essential to recognize that teachers are likely experiencing higher stress levels and lower job satisfaction than other school workers, notably head teachers and teaching assistants (Johnson, et at., 2005). That plays a significant role when thinking about how to leverage staff experience in a way that would lead to better school culture fit across all the involved parties.

School management should first and foremost focus their efforts on reducing stress levels and enhancing motivation by implementing flexible work schedules, committing to health and wellness, and clearly communicating the teacher's purpose and impact of their work.

Organization's across industry are replete with examples of employee dissatisfaction and burnout. Overworked and often underappreciated, employees can quickly become disillusioned with their work and significantly reduce their productive hours at work. Employees may be present in the office, but they are far from full engagement. Our schools cannot afford this outcome, especially because teachers directly influence the level of motivation and productivity of their students.

## How to Avoid Burnout

Christina Maslach has developed a framework of workload, control, reward, community, fairness and values to assess burnout at work. Maslach's framework is an "organizational effort" to both recognize burnout and to lower the severity of it (Maslach, 2018). Schools must look carefully at job demand and teacher's autonomy. In job demand, does the school place teachers in the right class that matches their skill level and temperament? In addition, school leaders should consider whether teachers feel significantly empowered to make meaningful decisions. Try to minimize the instances where teachers would feel overwhelmed and where they have very little control in their decisions. Provide autonomy and choice for teachers whenever possible. Overwhelmed and disempowered, they are more likely to experience burnout. This reality must be front of mind for school leaders. Both job demand and teacher's autonomy will directly impact staff experience.

## Why are my to-do lists only the beginning?

I (Marc) had a lot of to-do lists. I used to write a few things down, cross them off and look back and say, "Wow, I've just accomplished so much." In reality, I was accomplishing very little, least of all the most important stuff. According to Brian Tracy, the legendary self-help coach, in Eat that Frog, leaders need to prioritize their to-do lists (Berrett-Koehler, 2006).

By doing so, they can identify the "most important and hardest thing". Once a leader has identified the most important thing (M.I.T., not to be confused with the college), do the M.I.T. first, thus metaphorically "eating your frog" (and I am sure loving it!).

This concept was introduced earlier in the text as we examined the student experience and it has been reinforced in other classics such as The One Thing (Keller & Papasan, 2017) and The 7 Habits of Highly Effective People (Covey, 2016). Examples for teachers abound. For instance, teachers should never photocopy first thing in the morning. Something as small and trivial as photocopying could set the wrong rhythm for your entire day. All the redundant tasks are best completed at the end of the day when one is emotionally tired, and could complete some mindless tasks. Save the mornings for the important stuff, or perhaps the complex tasks that require full engagement. This concept should be familiar by now, since we used the same approach when discussing the student's daily schedule above.

Interestingly enough, science adds support to this notion of doing the most important thing first. Roy Baumeister, in his groundbreaking research on willpower depletion, put together two separate groups of participants, Group A and Group B (Mead et al., 2010). Each group was placed in their own room, aromatized with a scent of fresh-made chocolate chip cookies. Group A was given cookies. Group B, meanwhile, had to eat radishes (while having to cope with a scent of chocolate chip cookies!)

After finishing their "snacks", each group was given a difficult puzzle to complete. Group A, the group that was given cookies, stayed with the task 18 minutes longer than the group that ate radishes. Why such a drastic difference in results? Those who ate radishes made far fewer attempts and devoted less than half the time solving the puzzle compared to the chocolate-eating participants and a control group that only joined this latter phase of the study. In other words, those who had to resist the sweets and force themselves to eat pungent vegetables could no longer find the will to fully engage in another torturous task. They were already too tired.

Teachers will often have to exert their willpower to the point of exhaustion. However, we are human. And as such, we must recognize the finite quality of our daily energy, enthusiasm, and willpower. Bringing energy levels to zero by the end of the day has a cumulative effect on our long-term performance and motivation. This inevitably serves as an impediment to achieving school culture fit.

The key takeaway is this: Do the most important thing first, while you still have the willpower to endure it. Something as simple as photocopying at the end of the day will save time the next day and allow you to invest your morning efforts to important and high-impact tasks.

### *Enhanced Time Management*

*Marc's Story*

Some time management experts have gone as far as to advocate for getting rid of to-do lists altogether. Kevin Kruse, in *15 Secrets Successful People Know about Time Management*, suggests scheduling everything (Kruse, 2015). He reasons that successful and ultra-productive people schedule everything because time is the single one most valuable and scarce resource any person has. Imagine the tongue-in-cheek phrase, "have your people call my people". Kruse recommends working from your calendar, not the to-do lists, and he has a good point. Still, I kept finding myself not willing to discard my "to-do" list altogether - so I have combined both trains of thought.

I have a daily "to-do list" in which I write down everything that needs to be completed. I then prioritize the items on my list into three categories. First, I identify the most important task (M.I.T) of the day. Second, I decide upon "the important" tasks which remain in a prioritized category, if not an M.I.T. The third tranche is 'if I can get to it, cool.'

I then transfer my most important task (M.I.T) into my schedule first, adding the merely important things afterwards. Finally, if the "other items" can fit toward the end of the day, they get put into the schedule. If I can't get to these items, they remain on the to-do list for another day. These non-accomplished items are rarely crossed off from the list at the end of each day. Interestingly, many of these items simply go away, never reaching the level of importance that they formerly held.

I review my schedule for the next day before I go to bed at night and again in the morning. This way, I know I am in control of the day because I *designed* it.

Schedule /Day/Date

| | | | |
|---|---|---|---|
| 8 AM | | 8:30 AM | |
| 9 AM | | 9:30 AM | |
| 10 AM | | 10:30 AM | |
| 11 AM | | 11:30 AM | |
| 12 PM | | 12:30 PM | |
| 1 PM | | 1:30 PM | |
| 2 PM | | 2:30 PM | |
| 3 PM | | 3:30 PM | |
| 4 PM | | 4:30 PM | |
| 5 PM | | 5:30 PM | |
| 6 PM | | 6:30 PM | |
| 7 PM | | 7:30 PM | |

## *Free block, what free block?*

Many teachers have one "free block' a day to plan lessons or to simply catch up. During this time, teachers are often inundated with students asking questions or seeking additional instruction, disabling them to properly plan, and thus negatively influencing the performance. To facilitate this process, school leaders often utilize a so-called impromptu class, designed as a "free or planning" block. This gives structure to the day and enhances productivity of your staff members. Add to this, other tasks such as covering a colleagues' class, working on a school committee, or preparing for an after-school activity, and teachers start to wonder where the 'free block' went?

As a school leader, you should pay close attention to how teachers are planning their days since it directly impacts students. So often, teachers simply do not know how long it takes for them to prepare a lesson plan. This is where time management begins for teachers. School management should invest in facilitating the preparation process for lectures. A good practice is to assume that one week of lesson plans takes about 6 hours to prepare. Always advise your teachers to chunk the planning into smaller tasks, so teachers can maximize their creativity and delay exhaustion of willpower.

Jen Sincero, in *You Are Badass*, does a wonderful explanation of "chunking" and I suggest that all school leaders provide a copy to their teachers (Books, 2015). Furthermore, school leaders should search for best practices amongst their faculty. Are there teachers in the school who have unique expertise in this area or a creative approach to lesson planning? If so, consider creating venues for them to provide professional development for their peers.

So we now know how long it takes to finish a lesson plan. But how do we find the actual time during which to complete a lesson plan? School leaders should take into consideration the following calculation and devise best recommendations for their teachers. If a teacher has a 50 minute free block, say 12:00pm to 12:50pm, they could stick a sign on the door saying "office hours" are held from 12:30pm to 12:50pm. This provides a ½ hour block to complete part of your lesson plan. This time is for concentrated and undisruptive work. No emails, facebook, or texts during this time. What is needed, as Cal Newport puts it in his book titled, Deep Work, is focused, uninterrupted time to get into a "flow" or "the zone" to execute the awesome work (Newport, 2018).

If there is a school-wide redesign of what office hours are and how they are conducted, time management practices will be upgraded not only for the teachers, but for the students as well. Knowing the precise time allocated to get their questions answered, students will prioritize and streamline questions in a highly productive manner. In the end, it's all about taking control of what you can control, setting priorities, and designing your awesome school day for every person at your institution!

As school leaders, we must lead from a position of empathy. We must know what our teachers' pain points are. We understand what they need and desire. Though it may vary from school to school, there are specific needs that all teachers desire to be met:

### a. *Time for planning and grading assignments.*

Collaborative time with colleagues to design shared lessons within their own and cross-disciplinary departments.

### b. *Respect for the demands on their time.*

When possible, school leaders should reduce staff meeting time and frequency. Instead, share logistics through tools such as Google docs, Trello, Pear Deck, Asana, or any other applicable CRM (customer relationship management). At a minimum, school leaders should share agendas in advance and hold necessary conversations beforehand with critical stakeholders. This will shorten the time staff meetings require and also present a more organized picture for the principal or the team leader.

### c. *Flexibility in their time on campus.*

If a teacher needs to leave at 2:00pm on a specific day to fulfill a personal or family obligation, school leaders should make that option easily available to them. While early departures should not become a habit, school leaders must recognize the time teachers devote to grading, answering emails, and lesson planning in the evenings (a time when teachers are technically "off the clock"). As a result, responsible flexibility in terms of daytime commitments is appropriate and equitable.

# ESTABLISHING EMPLOYEE WELL-BEING

School leaders have a responsibility to maintain the well-being of their staff members. Consequently, we are obligated to pay careful attention to their overall wellness. *TotalWellness* founder and corporate wellness expert, Alan Kohll, emphasized the importance of employee wellness when designing the employee experience (Kohll, 2018). He urged organizations to engage in holistic wellness on behalf of their employees. In other words, beyond salary and benefits, what do employees want from their employer?

In a multi-year study of over 7,500 respondents, employees shared their desires (Global Talent Trends Study: Mercer 2020). It turns out, employees want to feel respected as a professional and an individual at their workplace. They also want their organizational contributions and their personal identities to be validated. Finally, employees desire to be respected for their unique qualities and life responsibilities. Organizing the survey results, Kohll distilled these findings into three tenets:

*Employees want flexible work schedules.* In the survey, 84% of working parents ranked flexible schedules as the most important factor in their job. Perhaps more than ever, working parents have an incessant stream of time commitments to attend to. Youth sports and community activities occur every weekend and several nights during the week, commutes are getting longer (many well over an hour), and caring for aging parents is becoming a more prominent responsibility for working adults. School leaders must recognize the impact of these commitments, and others, on the 'whole person' and understand that they do not employ robots; they employ people.

*Employees want a commitment to health and wellness on the part of their employer.* School management must demonstrate, through both policy and program, a genuine commitment to support employee wellness while at work. Examples could include providing healthy food options, flexible time during the day to allow for exercise, standing desks, and many others. Employees are now analyzing their jobs in relation to the demands it places on their lives. Often, they are as interested in the time demands the job will require as they are the salary it carries. Quality of life is of paramount concern - perhaps more than ever before. This is particularly relevant to teachers, as often their work extends beyond the typical work day.

*Employees want to identify a clear purpose for their work.* Staff members are asking themselves, "How am I contributing to society through my role?" As alignment between job responsibilities and purpose increases, so too does employee job satisfaction. Schools have a winning hand to play here. When it comes to purpose and impacting people, the work of educators enjoys powerful alignment. School management only has to clearly communicate that impact on school culture fit and emphasize community-wide recognition of the teacher.

# 4 OPPORTUNITIES TO DELIVER AN EXCEPTIONAL STAFF EXPERIENCE

## Professional Development

Every staff member should have a customized professional development plan that will help achieve growth, while benefiting both the teacher and the school (Guskey, 2000). Schools may consider formally incentivizing external certificates and badging programs. They may also create an internal model that would directly foster these benefits. Such certification and badging processes can be measured on a weekly, monthly, or semi-annual basis.

We are not referring to expensive conferences that interfere with schedules and can incur significant time and monetary costs. In fact, staff can achieve meaningful and effective professional development through online tools and the resources you have access to through the school. Collaboration with local institutions and fellow educators could also be an opportunity your staff could leverage for growth.

Other ideas include a monthly reading stipend. Staff members could be allotted $30.00 per month to purchase books or audio books. Audio books are an excellent source of professional development as they can transform commutes, exercise routines, or household activities into a mobile classroom. As staff members purchase a book, they simply take the receipt to the business office. The monthly expense is then credited to the staff member on the next payroll.

Independent and private schools truly have a unique opportunity to provide robust professional development. Independent and private schools are often destinations for educators who view themselves as artisans. These 'artisan educators' are intensely dedicated to their craft - they value their own growth in the field in comparable measure to incentives such as salary or other benefits. Remember, teachers of independent and private schools are not enrolled in a state retirement pension plan. Many of them chose the independent or private school route because it more closely aligned with their approach to education. Consequently, they often view their roles and responsibilities, perhaps even their careers, in a unique manner.

So, what does a robust professional development offering possibly look like? It could consist of the following:

a. Local conferences and Edcamps;
b. National and international conferences;
c. Reimbursement for online mini-courses;
d. Partial reimbursement for industry certificates, Master's and Doctoral-level degrees;
e. Non-monetary recognition for completing webinars and publishing scholarship;
f. Internal badging and micro-credentialing;
g. Monthly reading stipends.

There are countless additional possibilities. Providing professional development is an investment with a guaranteed return (Conzemius & O'Neill, 2002). This choice requires a strong commitment on the part of the Trustees and upper-level school leaders. Still, it is a necessary, strategic decision.

School leaders can increase talent retention through a robust professional development program. Always remember Henry Ford's words - "If you think investing in people and then having them leave is expensive, try not investing in them and having them stay." As a leader, you should be focused on long-term sustainability and organizational success factors. Employees who feel valued are more loyal to their employer. And teacher retention is of paramount importance to current and prospective parents.

# PERSONAL DEVELOPMENT

In addition, staff should have the access to personal development outlets. For example, if a teacher wants to run a triathlon, then the track coach can help train them. If a teacher wants to write their first novel, perhaps an English teacher can assist in the process. Not only would it allow employees to grow their skills and fulfil their interests, but also establish a collaborative environment within a co-learning space. A key consideration in this approach will be to ensure such collaboration occurs in a manner sensitive to the demands teachers face. Perhaps teachers join the conditioning aspects of an athletic team's training in the afternoon or audit a colleagues' statistics class. In addition, staff could collectively approach this type of collaboration by identifying and designating specific opportunities throughout the calendar year where peer to peer training and mentorship can take place.

Personal development can be a catalyst for community building and demonstrates to the faculty that the school cares about them personally. Celebrating your employees also matters. School leaders should formally recognize and applaud outstanding personal achievements in the lives of staff members. Motivated, excited, enthusiastic people become motivated, excited, and enthusiastic educators. It becomes a cultural norm. That way, students who interact within this forward-looking environment are inspired to explore their interests and take examples from their educators.

Not to mention that such a high-performing approach is especially attractive to current and prospective families. Think about your own life. Who do you want to be around - people who are thriving or people who are surviving? Families gravitate to the former and so do outstanding educators.

# Family Leave

Faculty and staff should be provided, and encouraged, to take substantial family leave for qualifying life events. One prominent example of such an event is the birth of a child. In a recent Fast Company article, Maurie Backman emphasized that few employees take advantage of this critical benefit (Visram, 2019). According to a report issued by Jobvite, "...63% of American workers say that parental-leave benefits are important to them...But surprisingly, only 21% of workers have ever taken parental leave offered by their employer." Too often, employees are afraid to be away from the office for a long period of time. There is an ingrained fear of losing position within the organization, missing on programs and events, and having to deal with the operational implications of temporary leave.

School leaders should place their prime attention on alleviating this tension and making sure to address the process of utilizing Paid Family Leave. Schools should not only include this option in the employee package, but also incorporate it as a normal and integral part of the culture. Why? Because the long-term benefits for the individual and the school far outweigh any short-term costs associated with the change and routine disruption.

*Matt's story*

Just a few years ago, I became a father. Having a child was, and continues to be, the most amazing, fulfilling experience in my life. And, it can also be quite exhausting.

As a brand new parent, I remember driving the car from the hospital, through the city of Frederick, Maryland, and arriving at our walk-up apartment downtown. I made sure every step of the way was clear for my wife, as I carried our little boy with the care of the nuclear football. It was truly exhilarating. I also remember that first night at home, with no support from the wonderful nurses at the hospital. Sleep was a distant friend. Anxiety ran high.

And that was my experience as a daddy. I had it easy compared to my wife's experience.

I took two weeks off. I could have taken more. But I had

recently accepted my first job as an Assistant Principal and I wanted to exceed all the expectations and prove my worth. My biggest fear was that the school would run well without me *(of course it would)* and everyone would decide I wasn't much needed at all. This was entirely self-inflicted, but emotionally draining nonetheless.

Citing a study by the Boston College Center for Work & Family, Backman suggested that I am not alone. "Taking time off for parental leave can be especially challenging for men due to the pressure or stigma involved...In fact, 76% of fathers take one week off or less following the birth or adoption of a child" (Expanded Paid Parental Leave Measuring the Impact of Leave on Work & Family, 2019). The research on parental leave is crucial to employee satisfaction, retention, and performance. Each scenario is unique and requires special attention from the upper management at the school, however the need for changing cultural perceptions around parental leave is uniform across the educational industry and beyond.

Looking back, I should have taken twelve weeks off. All my fears were, of course, nothing but the result of life changes topped with unnecessary assumptions. Years later, there is no lasting impact from any work I completed over those first ten weeks after my parental leave. At the same time, the lasting memories that could have been made at home with my wife and our newly born son, would most certainly carry on to this day.

I share this story not out of regret or bitterness. Quite the contrary, I greatly enjoyed an incredibly supportive environment at the Bullis School and continue to value my work there as a staff member. I was the one who initiated taking only two weeks off.

And that's the point. The most driven, ambitious, and often successful faculty and staff are most likely to return sooner than they should. Thus, school leaders have a responsibility to normalize taking twelve weeks off for the birth of a child. Taking personal and family time off from work, should be applauded and encouraged. The result will be a more healthy, stable, and inspired team, which will convert to a greater sense of loyalty and commitment to the school. You can't deny, that's a pretty good ROI.

# DELIVER AN EPIC EXPERIENCE

School leaders should work with their staff to ensure that every class, every interaction, every aspect of school life is an "EPIC" experience. In the *Power of Moments*, the authors discuss how to ensure that every moment is special and unique (Heath, 2019). Their EPIC rubric includes: 'elevate, pride, gain insight and build connections.'

Let's take a look at each step in the rubric. First, *elevated* experiences go beyond the predetermined routine. How can we go beyond our traditional class of power points or socratic methods? How can a classroom teacher make today's lesson a class students will remember? Consider the epic experience challenge from the lens of a Dining Hall staff member. How can they deliver an epic dining experience today for colleagues and students, alike?

To excel in *pride*, staff should focus on how to highlight student achievement. That way, students will feel confident in their ability to take on new challenges and embrace true ownership of their work. Students must clearly understand the difference between confidence and arrogance. Rewarding students should be implemented in an equitable and highly-challenging environment, where the assessment is based on the process, not the outcome.

Achieving *insight* is directly correlated with ensuring that students are able to explore their interests and are challenged daily by new learning experiences. In addition to teaching the curriculum, educators should try to distill all the potential insights and handpick those that they believe will most positively affect student's futures - reinforcing these at every opportunity.

And finally, how do we *build connections* to the world outside of the classroom, so that students feel they are a part of something bigger than themselves? Indeed, this is never an easy task.

However, developing the right environment for these meaningful connections to occur will facilitate the growth of student's networks and further their outreach to the real world.

# ABOVE ALL, CARE FOR YOUR EMPLOYEES

Always remember that your staff members expect you, first and foremost, to be fully committed to the school's purpose, mission, and vision. When the institution achieves school culture fit, staff are confident that the executive team understands their needs, fears, and aspirations. And with that knowledge, they hope you will be faithfully advocating for them and protecting their professional well-being.

Even if this holds true already, it is essential to communicate to your faculty and staff that their school team is their best advocate. Something as small as quick announcements, celebrations, and obtaining feedback at the weekly meetings will incite further commitment and loyalty to the school. And remember, what seems like a small gesture to you as a leader, may have an outsized impact on a colleague.

Consider the example of Naismith Hall of Fame Basketball Coach, Red Auerbach. Auerbach is widely considered to be one of the five greatest basketball coaches in history, winning 9 National Basketball Association (NBA) championships as Head Coach of the Boston Celtics. One of Auerbach's star players during this historical run was the great, Bill Russell.

In his book, *Red and Me: My Coach, My Lifelong Friend*, Russell paints a poignant portrait of Auerbach as his coach, leader, and friend. Russell shared that it was Auerbach's nonstop work on behalf of his players that earned the players' trust in him (Russell & Steinberg, 2010, p. 9). "It was like my father's admonition to give three dollards worth of work for two dollars pay - Red was giving us ten! And he recognized that it wasn't for him; it was all for his team. In his selfless devotion and loyalty to us, there was a measure of almost tender affection…" Consequently, Auerbach could be demanding of his players; he could require a lot from them. His players observed and felt his devotion to them and commitment to their well-being. And in return, they responded positively as their coach raised the bar of expectation.

Staff should feel that same appreciation and bond with their school's leadership team. If this bond is to be cultivated, staff members must be confident in the leadership team's commitment to them as individuals. Consider the following testimonial from an executive at *Chick-fil-A*. "The most important people in this business are our employees. Some people will say customers are most important, but if we create the right atmosphere for growth, they will get a kick out of their work. Then that feeling will spill right over to the customer" (Cathy, 2002). As team members see evidence of such a commitment to their well-being, organizational culture and performance prosper.

Indeed, managing people is often the most challenging task of any organization. Leaders should take all the measures necessary to not only optimize processes, but also approach every team member as an individual. Leaders must know the needs and expectations of each member of their team.

The same holds true for schools. Faculty and staff must be the first priority as it relates to school leadership decisions and governance. Students and their families are a close second. However, if a school's staff are not cared for, the education (service) provided to students and families will be suboptimal. As a school leader, you should be the most passionate advocates of your staff members.

7 Reflection Questions:
a. As a leadership team, how do you prioritize staff members?
b. Do you know what your staff values as professionals and individuals?
c. Is your school resourced to provide a realistic and sustainable teaching load?
d. Are staff members resourced to meet the challenges they face?
e. If this is not possible, how do you communicate to teachers the value you place on them?
f. Are there additional opportunities the community can leverage to encourage staff?

g. Does your strategic plan emphasize staff development, individually and corporately?

Ultimately, staff members deserve to have confidence that the school's leadership team understands the challenges they are facing and are constantly exerting efforts to support them. Such is the staff experience when school culture fit is achieved.

# PARENT EXPECTATIONS

Parent expectations refer to the outcomes and the environment parents hope their children will experience while at school. These are especially helpful when you are determining how to improve your school and what to focus on when talking to prospective families.

| | |
|---|---|
| *Functional jobs-to-be-done* | To demonstrate to parents that their students are learning meaningful content, while developing both the soft and hard skills |
| *Emotional jobs-to-be-done* | To establish a school culture that is warm, inclusive, and challenging where all students experience productive relationships across campus life. |
| *Social jobs-to-be-done* | To connect parents to their child's journey in the school, while identifying the programs that ensure this parent-school relationship remains vibrant and collaborative. |

If schools are to excel and enjoy a healthy school culture fit, leaders must have a strong knowledge of the expectations of their parent community and exceed those expectations. Parent expectations are fulfilled by, and congruent to, the school's purpose. Parents know that their students are learning meaningful content, while developing both the soft and hard skills needed to thrive once they enter the real world.

In deciding which school to choose, parents prioritize learning about a potential school's shared values, the stated curriculum, and what skills students will acquire during the learning process. Too often, schools communicate particular reasons as to why students should attend, while failing to deliver upon these stated outcomes. The school's value-proposition becomes aspirational, as opposed to a documentation of the student experience. The school then anchors itself to *who we wish we were vs. who we are.*

Schools must achieve alignment between what the school claims and the outcomes they deliver for students. This shared value approach, i.e., to achieve school culture fit, should be measured carefully by the school. Below are four metrics to measure and ensure that school culture fit is achieved. These metrics can be approached as commitments the school makes to parents in return for entrusting the school with their child(ren).

# Progress Principle

Progress principle allows parents to track student performance. Student progress must be transparent and easily observed (Amabile & Kramer, 2011). Parents are often unable to discern how much progress a student is making. Generally, students are given a report card at the end of the trimester or semester, supplemented by regularly occurring interims. Grades, however, do not track the daily learning that occurs for the student.

Educators should shift the emphasis from an end-of-trimester/term/semester grade to a daily progress report of content and skills acquisition. We are suggesting putting in metrics that can be gauged on a daily and weekly basis. In fact, if a student were to progress merely 1% a week, after a year they would be 50% better off then at the start of school.[3] This approach of small, incremental steps towards advancement is also an effective means to gain confidence. Overall, daily progress will remind students to celebrate their successes. It will help educators to attend to the setbacks and deal with them quickly. Teachers will be aware of what is and is not working which would allow teachers to address the issues early on, thus preventing large learning gaps from taking root.

---

[3] The compound effect would yield around 300% in actual rate of improvement.

## Community

Parents represent a critical stakeholder group for schools. As a result, they should feel like full members of the school community. Indeed, parents play a pivotal role in the school community and are a vital component of achieving school culture fit. The focus of school personnel and parents, of course, is the students. Parents should attend a certain number of sports and/or cultural events. They should be active participants in service learning, field trips, and holiday celebrations. An enriched community, however, confers benefits upon parents of being part of the "network" outside of the school walls. This can be in the form of student internships, discounts at their place of work, or mentorship opportunities. In other words, the school community offers parents value as well (Brooks, 2011).

At the time of writing, we also advise school leaders to consider the challenges of social distancing in the era of COVID. You should identify the local challenges that result due to a lack of social engagement and then use this to create a school that reveres connection.

Being part of the community can even begin prior to the application process. Parents should be made aware of the many opportunities to be involved in the school's community. Before enrolling their child, prospective parents recognize the school as a 'family school' - one that adds value in direct proportion to the value parents choose to add to it. Parents get the feel that they are not just getting a school but a unique, value-driven community.

## Mentorship

As part of the community, parents will have access to mentorship and learning opportunities. With the ever changing marketplace, businesses cannot remain stagnant. Therefore, organizational leaders must recognize the need for a life-long commitment to learning. As a part of the community, if a parent voices the desire to improve or acquire new skills, they could be paired with another parent or alumni with expertise in that particular area. Schools may determine on their own if this service is an additional fee-based service.

In either case, parents must be able to see the benefit of being part of the community and mentorship is certainly one way to convey that sense of belonging. As an added benefit, formalizing a mentorship program to benefit parents will continually connect bridges across your community, thereby building the school network further, and strengthening your school culture fit.

## Parent Ambassador

The parent community should serve as brand ambassadors for the school. As such, schools need to generate excitement within the community, and provide possible incentives to ensure that parents continue to promote the school. Considering recent studies, it is clear that many people base their decisions on personal referrals (Chedid, 2018). Word-of-mouth marketing is becoming even more lucrative and powerful as the advertising clutter only increases. Parents should serve as passionate, front-line ambassadors for the school community and its efficacy. Parents know how well their child is interacting with the school. They also know if other families would be a good fit for the community. As a result, parents should be leveraged in assessing the culture fit of prospective families, validating the work of the school to families throughout the admission process, and serving as resources for admitted families who are making final enrollment decisions.

Some schools may want to consider referral recommendation fees from families for prospective students. This is an optional measure that is entirely up to school management to implement. If nothing else, such a fee may serve as a token of appreciation for the valuable role a current family filled in the decision process of an applicant family. Your recognition will signal the appreciation you have for your parent community and in return, can further increase their commitment to the school.

# SCHOOL ECOSYSTEM

School ecosystem refers to anyone within the extended community of the school. That is, those who are not regularly present on campus throughout the school day. Parents and alumni for example, as well as other stakeholders, are integral to how your school is presented in the broader community.

| | |
|---|---|
| *Functional jobs-to-be-done* | To connect every stakeholder to the school's ecosystem through experiences that add personal, life-long value |
| *Emotional jobs-to-be-done* | To make every stakeholder feel connected to the school community |
| *Social jobs-to-be-done* | To recognize every stakeholder's unique contribution to the ecosystem |

The school's ecosystem extends beyond the school walls. This ecosystem provides tangible benefits to students, parents, staff, and alumni as they have an opportunity to leverage the collective network of their school community. The school experience is a fundamental period in life and should have its privileges.

In order to maximize the collaborative network, schools need a systematic approach to bridge the gap between the students, parents, and alumni, forming one single community with a shared purpose. This is the value of the ecosystem - it connects people, while synergizing energy, connections, resources, ideas, and school spirit. Together then, your school can communicate to the outside world who you are as a school community and what your school stands for.

There are many components and tactical approaches a school can take to fully develop its ecosystem. Once the shared purpose is established and widely approved, you can proceed to include the practices below:

# Internships and Jobs

Employers indicated the strongest determinatives of success in the workplace are emotional intelligence and internship experience (Goldstein, 2017; Busteed & Auter, 2020). As a result, schools should prioritize the implementation and execution of a sustainable internship program. For example, each division of the school should have different experiences for student internships. Middle School internships should be designed for mere exposure, as opposed to more experiential internships in the Upper School. In theory, the Middle School student internships can be conducted through simulations rather than the physical hands-on workplaces.

In the Upper School, however, internships should be actual experiences where students will have the ability and means to pursue areas of interest. The internship program employs a systematic approach where students can test and truly experience the many fields that your geographic region has to offer.

As part of the internship system, parents can be actively engaged and may very well provide many of these experiences. As a result, there is a reciprocity and a benefit effect for parents as well. Providing internships for talented students can boost a company or organization's standing within the school ecosystem, provide for parent to parent networking, while also serving as a long-term talent recruitment opportunity. Perhaps a talented student will fondly remember his/her internship, and after college or graduate school, accept a full-time position with the same company or organization. In essence, parents should have the ability to tap into this network to provide not only internships for their children, but for their own companies and organizations as well.

Most importantly, a strong internship program helps ensure that students will be better prepared for the job market. Internships for students provide an opportunity to apply knowledge gained in the classroom in a hands-on environment. Internships also serve to connect students with the parent and alumni community. These internship opportunities are generally offered during the summer months. The benefit is twofold; first, the students are able to gain meaningful experience and also strengthen their college application. Second, students have the ability to experience various industries and identify their professional interests. For example, a student may be interested in studying medical engineering in college. However, the application process is extremely competitive for engineering majors.

By having students first gauge their true interest in that field during high school, they are equipped with a stronger understanding of what they want to study. Students are also afforded the opportunity to discover if there are other career paths they feel inclined to pursue. If during the internship the student discovers that engineering is not a true passion, he/she will have the time and resources to continue searching for other alternatives.

For parents and alumni in the community, internships are an opportunity to contribute their expertise to the student body. By recruiting students, they are securing an immense added benefit to the school, to the intern, and to their business organization. Schools may also manage this internship program using well-established tools like Thrively.

The internship model can be an especially powerful tool for schools located in, or near, urban centers. For example, Bullis School is located in Potomac, MD. Our students live throughout the Washington D.C. Metro area. As a result, Bullis students have access to one of the most robust job markets in the world. From industry, non-profit, to government, opportunities for students to engage in the professional world are endless. Leveraging the internship opportunity is a win for all stakeholders in your school community. Finally, schools that have a geographic advantage have a subsequent responsibility to leverage the opportunity on behalf of their students, families, and the school's position in the marketplace.

## Professional Network

The benefits of the community must reach beyond the school-based student experience, adding value to the student even after they graduate. Often, former students will find themselves in transition from one job to another. In fact, millennials and Generation Z may have as many as 7 to 9 different jobs during their lifetime (Ripplematch, 2018). A former student in their 30s or 40s may have interests beyond his or her prior fields and may decide to join a completely different venture. Current alumni and parents can open up many doors and promising possibilities to this former student. As a school leader, you could set this up in a form of an internal school referral program to help your alumni obtain new jobs. With the onset of Covid 19 and the lingering effects of a tighter job market, networking, and connection to potential jobs will become more and more important for your graduates as they seek jobs.

## Community First

There are many jobs in a school environment which require outside vendor support. Normally, there is a Requests for Proposals (RFPs) process whereby potential businesses bid on opportunities for jobs at that school. There are more opportunities in this process than you could imagine. With this in mind, you should definitely consider giving the first priority of choice to the parent and alumni network, allowing them to offer services to the community they are part of. For example, a facilities cleaning job should be offered first to a parent's company before seeking any outside vendor. We are not advocating the school not obtain bids on work from multiple companies, or hire sub-par vendors. Instead, schools should be intentional as it relates to building community in every way possible. And when a need can be met by a community member - through an excellent product or service and fair pricing - schools have an opportunity to both align interests and invest in their own community.

## College Connection

The college application process has become more competitive as the incoming pool of students continues to raise standards. Your students will most likely apply to more than 15 schools in order to maximize their chances of obtaining admission to desirable institutions. However, more often than not, they have no understanding of the community they are applying to and what the campus life is like.

In response, the school community should offer a wide range of resources to improve a better fit and success for the student during their college application process. The alumni and parent community could provide detailed insights that a one-day visit simply cannot cover. Moreover, alumni parents can help in the process to secure a successful application to a particular university.

For example, if a student wanted to attend Duke University, alumni could help in two ways. First, they can provide the ins-and-outs of what Duke University was actually like during their years at the school. Second, as an alumnus of both the university and your school, they may be able to assist in the application process and drafting college essays. If available, every student should be paired with an alumni of a desired university to get a sense of the university and to help them make connections and possibly secure recommendations to that university.

# Referral fee

A referral fee signals to the community that alumni parents and teachers play an integral role in the admission process and in building the community. A referral fee also recognizes that families and faculty are our best brand ambassadors. One approach of "signaling" to them could be a bonus to faculty and alumni or a tuition credit for bringing in a new family or new faculty member to the school community. Another approach is credit at the school store, or other incentives that signal to them that their contribution is appreciated. It is important to remember that appreciation does not need to come in monetary form. You could simply spotlight their contribution at a school-wide meeting or feature their support in a campus newsletter. Any recognition will only make your active community members more connected to the school.

## Mentorship

*Success leaves clues* is a phrase regularly cited in the business world. As is often the case, many in the school community have a certain expertise that they are willing to share with others. Stakeholders beyond the parent community can mentor and add value to students and to the school. In the school scenario, when we think of mentorship, we normally are only considering the student-adult relationship. However, in a strong community this mentorship model can extend to an adult-adult relationship.

In structuring this mentorship program, there is an initial vetting process of parents and alumni to become mentors. The approval process is designed to learn more about the community and gather expectations. Once approved, community members are placed in the system as an expert in that particular field. Members of the community, at this point, now have access to mentorship in whatever field they are seeking guidance in. The program will then pair interested students with the mentors in the field they need the most help in. For example, if a student is interested in piano, school leaders should pair the student with a pianist in the community to facilitate the learning process and inspire continued growth.

## First Access

Parents should be provided first access to RFP's and other vendor contracts through the school. Parents should also be extended extra benefits listed below in the "Community" section. Independent and private schools are complex operations and rely on a number of vendors for their operation. Vendors are needed for cleaning services, lawn services, painting projects, as well as other jobs in facilities. School leaders should consider offering the first set of RFP's to the parents of their community. Regardless of the school's ultimate choice on these bids, parents will feel more connected to, and recognized by, the school executive team. Not only will such an approach lead to higher parent satisfaction, but will also allow you to offer services that truly match parent expectations. The sense of belonging will increase the commitment level of parents to the school community, while their expertise in the areas you seek will prove important to your school's successful operation both in the short-term and long-term.


## Discounts

A strong school community has access to business relationships that can offer additional benefits to its members. Families and faculty should be able to receive discounts/cash backs at banks, restaurants, lawyer's offices, dentists and from other businesses and professionals in the school's network. The amount of the discount is at the discretion of the proprietor and it's not a requirement to become a member of the community. Such benefits serve as proof that a parent or alumni is a member of a thriving school community, from which they can receive tangible benefits extending beyond the school setting. Moreover, recipients will be more inclined to reciprocate and offer a generous discount or service as well.


## Affinity Programs

Amazon has established a strong affinity system whereby members of a school can order products off their website and the school receives a small portion of that sale. School leaders should consider extending this affinity program to other business opportunities within the community. For purchases made within the school community, part of the proceeds could go to development efforts such as the annual fund or the endowment (Bakhtiari, 2013).

# SCHOOL LEADER'S ACCOUNTABILITY

School leader's accountability refers to the responsibility you hold as an administrator. As a leader, your actions have a tremendous impact on the success of your school community. This responsibility must be acknowledged and embraced.

| | |
|---|---|
| *Functional jobs-to-be-done* | To hire talented and skilled individuals who provide school culture fit; to empower them to do the job |
| *Emotional jobs-to-be-done* | To improve and enhance school community well-being |
| *Social jobs-to-be-done* | To establish cross-departmental transparency; to divide accountability between your staff members |

## Hiring

A colleague of mine (Marc) had been recently hired to become a professor at a local university. His first day at work, there was no orientation, no expectations as to what a successful outcome was. Though empowered to find his place, he felt rudderless in the position. He quit three months later. For many, hiring is a nebulous endeavor with varying degrees of success. Hiring and retention for school culture fit is a process.

Though difficult, school leaders can ensure the right person is hired and that the employee has true job satisfaction for talent retention. The process consists of the following steps:

- Conduct a job analysis before posting the position
- Hire talented and skilled employees who fit your school culture

- Set clear expectations for the hire during the onboarding process
- Develop a goal setting process for both professional and personal goals of the employee once hired
- Develop a culture of feedback and psychological safety
- Establish a mentoring program for all team members
- Convert your school into a learning factory with the best professional development in the market

There is an old adage in the coaching world. It goes something like this: "Jimmy's and Joe's win more games than X's and O's." The point is that the best strategy and most effective plays a coach can implement are less powerful than the impact of great players. As a former basketball coach (Matt), I can testify that indeed, sometimes great players overwhelm great coaching. So what does this mean for schools? Simply put, school leaders must hire talented staff members. These high-talent individuals have the tools needed to drive tremendous student growth. However, schools must also ensure they hire for school culture fit.

Harkening back to my experience as a basketball coach, it is also true that talented teams can fail miserably. Why? If the culture of the team is not healthy, if there is not a culture fit, the talent will not coalesce into a cohesive unit. Talent alone is not enough. As leadership expert Jon Gordon shared, "Character and culture drive talent towards greatness" (Twitter, 2019). Thus, school leaders must ensure they hire staff members who are high-character, create and nurture an organizational culture which aligns with their stated values, and emphasizes collaborative achievement.

## *Job Analysis*

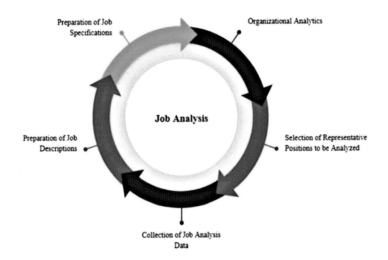

Each job has three core competencies: core task proficiency; the employee demonstrated effort; and maintenance of personal discipline (Conte & Landy, p. 153). A job analysis is important because based on the job analysis, school leaders will be able to "provide pre assignment and post assignment training opportunities (p. 172). In addition, school leaders need to discover for each job what Knowledge and Skills are needed as well as the Ability and Other Characteristics needed for the job (p. 108). Pivoting to the job analysis, the more inputs of data the better. As such, school leaders will observe the jobs, conduct qualitative interviews of supervisors and teachers, review critical incidents and work diaries, conduct and review surveys, and actually perform the job (pp. 177-178). These five steps will result in a deeper understanding of the role itself.

Moreover, culture fit is an important criteria for hiring, even if the potential employee has the skill set to do the job well, school leaders must ask "Does the teacher fit the culture and believe in the school's purpose?"

# Clear Expectations and Onboarding

## *Talent Retention.*

Hiring is just the first step in maintaining an excellent school culture fit. Schools retain their talent by developing and aligning organizational goals to personal goals, establishing clear expectations, empowering faculty, and developing a strong feedback loop that goes beyond the mere annual review. In addition, schools must ensure they are aligning their actions and the deployment of resources to their core values, vision, and mission.

## *Goal Setting.*

According to Conte and Landy, "The notion of a goal as a motivational force has been well established" (p. 328). Goal setting theory is a framework that considers the following:

1. How difficult is the goal?
2. How specific is the goal?
3. How committed is the employee to the goal?
4. Did the employee participate in setting the goal?
5. Does the employee receive feedback on their progress? (Locke & Lantham, 2005).

Prior to establishing their own goals, school employees should have a clear understanding of the organizational goals of the school. Moreover, organizational goals must go beyond just numbers. They must be school purpose driven, and the goals must be pervasive throughout the entire organization. Gartenberg and Serafeim observed, "The link between purpose and profitability is present only if senior management has been successful in diffusing that sense of purpose further down in the organization, especially in middle management, and in providing strategic clarity throughout the organization on how to achieve that purpose" (Gartenberg & Serafeim, 2016). In addition, Patrick Lencioni challenges leaders to remain committed to, and enthusiastic about, communicating organizational purpose and values. Lencioni suggests many leaders simply fail to sufficiently evangelize their message - citing studies indicating that organizational leaders must communicate a message as many as seven times before team members truly embrace it (Lencioni, 2020).

Consider the case of Alcoa, a struggling aluminum company with declining sales and a demoralized workforce. The new CEO came into Alcoa and instituted a safety first policy. A policy where every employee was held to the same standard, a policy that was pervasive through the entire organization. For example, if a manager was spotted on the floor without a helmet, any employee could tell the manager to wear a safety helmet or he was not permitted to go any further. In fact, it became so embedded that Alcoa employees were known to help strangers on the side of the road change their tire, the correct, safe way (Duhigg, 2012). At Alcoa, the organizational goal of safety became 'an every employee goal'. For schools, an embedded purpose goal can become 'an every employee goal' as well.

In applying this framework, once organizational goals are identified, school employees must be empowered to choose their own goals. As Conte and Landy note, "When the individual is free to revise assigned and accepted goals, they become self-set goals, thereby transforming what was once acceptance into commitment" (Conte & Landy, p. 329). In addition, by empowering school staff to set their own goals, staff feel more autonomous. Autonomy leads to less stress at work and more productivity (Conte & Landy, p. 414). In customizing the personal goals, we also recognize that each staff member has different attributes that they bring to the school (Conte & Landy, p. 90).

### *Feedback Loop.*

Many schools utilize annual performance reviews, yet are often left with little to show for It. Such reviews can quickly become just another 'box to check' before the school year ends. The review process can quickly become a logistical requirement as opposed to an opportunity for growth. Instead, a more holistic, "360" approach is recommended and is the modern trend of many organizations. In support, Denisi and Pirtchard noted that "employees should be evaluated in terms of increased productivity and performance, as well as customer satisfaction, learning, and growth within the organization" (DeNisi, A., & Pritchard, R., 2006). For teachers, consistent feedback from students, parents, peers, and administration are valuable in providing a holistic picture of the teacher's performance.

Managers enter a "feedback loop" where they can interact with employees to help them achieve their goals (Conte & Landy, p. 330). Good organizations have transitioned from limited annual reviews to more frequent interactions with the employee through a feedback loop. Organizations such as "General Electric Co, Microsoft Corp, The Goldman Sachs Group Inc, and Netflix Inc are ditching the long-standing tradition of annual performance appraisals and moving towards providing more frequent feedback on performance so that employees can quickly incorporate that information and respond in a timely manner" (Casas-Arce, P., & Martínez-Jerez, A., 2018).

Schools should transition school leaders and department chairs from merely annual reviewers of teachers, to active coaches in this feedback loop. Converting school leaders from managers to coaches, who consistently work with teachers for self guided improvement, will have a powerful effect on school performance (Conte & Landy, p. 302). This shift from evaluator to coach can also have a powerful impact on school culture.

By utilizing the daily huddles discussed below, supervisors enter a daily and weekly feedback loop with their teachers and staff members. The daily huddle is the daily feedback loop, which then culminates in the weekly accountability check in. During the accountability check in, the supervisor should be primarily listening to individual teachers. Through active listening, supervisors are then able to effectively equip and empower teachers and staff to achieve their goals (Conte & Landy, p. 330).

Clearly, despite engaging in this continual feedback loop, there are times when the supervisor needs to provide corrective action. In the past, the "sandwich technique" was utilized to provide negative feedback. This approach "sandwiched" negative feedback between two positive, feedback responses. Unfortunately, the sandwich technique has proven to be ineffective, as the employee tends to only remember the negative aspects of the conversation (Bressler, M. et. al, 2014).

In actuality, for every negative feedback, four instances of positive feedback are needed to overcome it (Tierney, J., & Baumeister, R., 2019).

When negative feedback is given, we recommend the following:
 a. negative feedback be given first;
 b. feedback is specific;
 c. correctable action and next steps are provided;
 d. follow up negative feedback with four positive feedback comments.

The feedback loop's success is in large measure dependent upon the relationship between both parties - supervisor and team member. When trust is present, and team members feel valued, they will be receptive to feedback. Consequently, this ongoing, authentic, and transparent approach to coaching vs. managing is able to flourish.

## *Expectations.*

Expectancy theory states that an employee is motivated by three interconnected factors. First, the employee must see a causal connection between their effort and performance, an "expectancy" that their effort will produce an outcome of sufficient value. Second, there must be a linkage between their performance and rewards, termed as "instrumentality". And finally, the reward has "valence" i.e., the reward must be worth the work required to achieve it (Hitt, pp. 186-187). These factors highlight the importance of giving teachers a clear pathway to a well-defined metric of "success".

School leaders must learn how to interact with their team on a daily basis and to set clear expectations. In American football, players meet before every play. Consequently, each player knows his role and task for that particular play. In addition, the entire team is striving for one goal - to reach the end zone. For schools, a similar format called a "daily huddle" (Harnish, 2014) can be used. In the daily huddle, each employee lays out his/her task for the day and communicates if they need any assistance in achieving that task. This format enables employees to honestly assess their day and to seek out guidance and assistance for troubled areas. In order for a daily huddle to function properly, teachers and staff members must have clear expectations of what they want to achieve for the day, that their effort will reap rewards, and that their environment is primed for success ( Conte & Landy, p. 275).

## Daily Huddle

Every team meets daily to assess organizational and personal goals. These short meetings are known as a "Daily Huddle." At the meetings, a scorecard of individual and organizational metrics to measure success will be utilized. As a team, this spreadsheet will be evaluated, and together, the team will work on improving performance. This process will enable you to prioritize the tasks for the day and oversee the progress of the team. Moreover, this daily discipline will help you avoid miscommunication (Harnish, 2014). The supervisor asks the employee four basic questions - what is the most important thing you want to achieve today, what is the constraint that is holding you back from achieving it, once the most important thing is solved, what is next in the process and then finally, as a supervisor, how can I help?

## Daily Huddle (7-10 minutes max)

| | | |
|---|---|---|
| Most Important Thing | What is THE thing that must get done today? | |
| Constraint | What is the bottleneck that prevents you from accomplishing it? | |
| Next Best Step | What should be the next step in the process? | |
| What do you need from me? | What can the school leader do to expedite the process in support of direct reports? | |

# Weekly 'Admin' Meeting

During your weekly 'admin' meeting, you should always follow the same meeting framework. The weekly meeting always begins at the same time, on time, and ends on time. At Facebook, Sheryl Sandberg would famously put a clock timer on the table during the meeting to ensure the meeting would not go past the designated time (Tett, G. 2013). For organizations and individuals, time is our most precious resource. Using it wisely and in a disciplined manner is not only 'good for business' but it sends a message of competence and strength across the leadership team as well. Thus, school leaders should stick to the meeting's designated time frame. Besides, school leaders should be out in the school, engaging with teachers and students, not getting stuck in meetings (Lencioni, 2004).

Each 'admin' meeting will have specific tasks and time slots so that all team members are aware of the meeting workflow. In addition, all members should receive a copy of the agenda two days prior to the meeting so that they are fully prepared and able to participate during the meeting. Here are the predetermined sections which will be included at every meeting:

### Positive achievement

Before the meeting turns to the specific agenda items, the facilitator should ask each participant to cite a positive achievement for the week. This puts the team in the right frame of mind. Professor Barbara Frederickson, from University of North Carolina, suggests that by starting with positivity, you actually turn the creative juices on. If a member cannot lead with a positive achievement that week, it is a clear indicator that they are not achieving their metrics.

### To do list review

This list is based on the previous week's meeting. The progress on previously assigned tasks is assessed and recommendations/reflections are made.

### Rock review

What are the three "rocks'" or the most important things that were mutually agreed on at the beginning of the trimester, term, or semester. These "rocks" need to be reviewed weekly and are tailored to each department. For example, it could be admissions or school culture, but you need to make sure that the focus is primarily on the aspects that directly help the school to thrive.

### Issue-Discuss-Solve

This is the most important part of the meeting, during which you discuss pressing student, faculty, parents, alumni and community issues. Together with the team, you can strategically approach these concerns and find most optimal solutions.

### Next Steps

Discuss assignments that each member of the team is receiving, as well as the date by which the assignments will be completed. This accountability chart is posted and will be available to review in real time. We recommend utilizing technology such as Google docs.

### Emergency Plan

Once a month, you will be reviewing your plan to make sure your system of checks and balances is working as intended under all the possible scenarios. Schools must be prepared for the worst - from safety and security emergencies, human resources issues, sharp economic downturns, to public health emergencies. For example, the COVID-19 crisis is forcing schools to grapple with challenges previously considered unfathomable. We suggest that you "rehearse" different hypothetical situations to prepare yourself and the relevant team to handle various crises and convey the appropriate messages to the community.

### Pre-Mortem meetings

A premortem is a meeting that occurs prior to the launch of the project. It hypothetically assumes that the project has occurred and has failed. As Gary Klein writes, "The team members' task is to generate plausible reasons for the project's failure" (Klein, 2014). As a leader, you may also say "the initiative failed, what went wrong?" By acknowledging the possibility of failure and understanding that unforeseen changes are inevitable, you and your team can plan accordingly to avoid these pitfalls. Additionally, identifying contingencies ensures that your team will be better able to anticipate and counteract these potential failures (Wickman, 2012).

This meeting agenda provides predictability and consistency to your leadership team, while facilitating clear expectations and communication. By including these points in your meeting agenda, you will be able to strategically leverage the time invested in the meeting and allocate resources to their greatest use. Further, your team will engage in coherent and measured problem-solving, while prioritizing the strategic planning process.

|  | Monday | Tuesday | Wednesday | Thursday | Friday | Objectives and Key Results |
|---|---|---|---|---|---|---|
| Week 1 Employee Goal: |  |  |  |  |  |  |
| School Goals |  |  |  |  |  |  |

# Environment

### Psychological safety

Staff and faculty may feel uncertain about the new goal setting policy or their job security in general. Such uncertainty is likely to become a hindrance to staff and faculty bringing their best selves to their work. In fact, psychological safety is a foundational component of life and work (Maslow, 1943). Though much of the prepotency elements of Maslow's theory have been refuted (Wahba & Bridwell, 1976), psychological safety has been proven to be an important element to work motivation (Schneider, 2016). So how do employees feel safe at school? The key is in the rewards.

### Rewards

In studying the struggles of organizations and how rewards helped turn the organization around, we can turn to the recent success of Ford. In the mid 2000s, Ford was teetering on bankruptcy until they brought in executive Alan Mulally to lead the company (Hoffman, 2012). One of Alan Mulally's first steps was to set up a business plan review system. Essentially, department goals are color coded; green if everything is going well and on target, yellow if there are some struggles but the team knows how to fix it; and red if their department needs assistance.

During the first meeting with his managers to implement this new business plan review system, remarkably, every manager had their team goals marked as green even though Ford was close to bankruptcy. Mulally quickly came to realize that the previous Ford culture had made the environment "unsafe" to admit problems. In disbelief, he sent the team away until the following week for the next team meeting. During the next team meeting, everyone came with green again except for one manager, whose board was red. All of the managers turned to that individual, assuming that he was going to get fired but instead, Mulally rewarded that individual with a promotion and spotlighted his courage to come forward with problems. Soon after, honesty and openness became a defining aspect of the Ford culture. It's this type of culture that schools must cultivate and ultimately systematize.

# Transforming School for School Culture Fit

Change in any organization can be a challenge. Schools are certainly no exception. In leading change across the school community, leaders must engage multiple stakeholders, while managing the uncertainty, fear, consternation, and general unease accompanying change in any context. Consequently, we suggest utilizing the following methodology:

| *unfreezing* | *changing* | *refreezing* |
|---|---|---|

The unfreezing, changing, refreezing methodology provides school leaders with a powerful framework from which to enact meaningful and sustainable change.

### Unfreezing for Teachers

During the unfreezing stage, school leaders must accomplish the following:

a. provide a rationale for the change;
b. create minor levels of guilt/anxiety about not changing;
c. create a sense of psychological safety to make the change (Hitt, 1999, p. 458).

The private and independent school industry faces significant headwinds and troubling market trends. Many schools find themselves in a precarious state as it relates to their marketplace viability as an institution. The onset of the coronavirus and the current financial crisis raises the question: Is the current model for independent schools sustainable? In order to offset this insecurity for teachers, schools need to provide a sense of urgency - one that underscores the reality that change is needed and that teachers and administrators are working together, vigorously, towards institutional success. Viewed this way, change is not what should be feared. Instead, a lack of change is the subject of fear - because it likely leads to a negative outcome for the school.

### Changing for Teachers

In the changing stage, the school needs to provide information that supports the reason for the change, remove obstacles for change, and bring about actual shifts in a change of behavior (Hitt, p. 458). School staff need to be reassured that the school cares for their well-being. As a school leader, you must remember the preeminence of Maslow's Hierarchy of Needs, where psychological safety plays an important role. In the school's purpose, school leaders and staff have a locus of focus and can work to remove any obstacles that detract from that focus..

### Refreezing for Teachers

The refreezing stage allows for the institutionalizing of systems and processes to support the behaviors in the organization. In this stage, schools must track behavior, rewards systems, and install a hiring and promotion system that supports the new behaviors.

School leaders can accomplish this phase by establishing the change into practice. Hands-on application of the learned skill will reinforce the change (Conte & Landy, p. 285). The leadership team must be transparent to students, parents, and the community at large, while modeling the changes in behavior, process, or protocol. This begins with the Head of School, her/his executive team, and applies to leaders throughout the school community. Accountability is not always an easy virtue to live up to. And yet, keeping it at the top of any organization is paramount to organizational performance and maintaining school culture fit.

## Total Accountability

The role of school leaders is to develop systems and processes to ensure school culture fit, as well as to ensure that student and faculty growth occurs in a well-balanced school environment. Best in class systems and processes have accountability built into the metrics. In order to establish school culture fit, the school leaders must be held accountable to measurable outcomes.

Indeed, successful and sustainable leadership requires a culture of accountability. And schools who achieve school culture fit embrace accountability as part of their ethos. In short, people must accept responsibility for their own performance and the outcomes produced within their teams.

School leaders must model accountability as part of their leadership framework. Angela Kambouris, CEO of Kambouris Consultancy, agreed, "To break through a blame and shame mentality, leaders must acknowledge their part of the problem. The leader sets the example for others to look in the mirror. When leaders acknowledge their mistakes, an accountability culture is bred where people hold themselves accountable irrespective of the level of authority."

To be sure, accountability is not an easy concept. The word does not conjure up warm thoughts and pleasant nostalgia. The truth is, most people do not readily embrace accountability. When things go bad, it is all too easy to blame other people or circumstances. While this is understandable, and to be clear, people often face trials and challenges to no fault of their own, the function of leadership demands an embrace of accountability, in order to maximize the individual productivity of each team member involved.

In fact, leaders must take *total accountability* for the success of the organization as a whole and team members as individuals. Accountability is *all or nothing*. A leader cannot be *sort of* accountable. They do not *dip their toes* in the *accountability pool*. Instead, effective leaders are *totally* accountable.

What exactly does accountability equate to in the organizational context? Leadership expert Michael Hyatt suggested, "First and foremost, it means that you accept responsibility for the outcomes expected of you - both good and bad. You don't blame others." Thus, accountability requires an active approach to leadership. Organizational outcomes are the result of the leader's actions or choices.

Hyatt continued, "Until you take responsibility, you are a victim. And being a victim is the opposite of being a leader" (2012). Leaders do not look externally for a blame target when results are disappointing or objectives are missed. They only look inwards. Hyatt identified four key actions *accountable* leaders take:

1. Accountable leaders own their role and influence by using the 'I' pronoun;
2. Accountable leaders clearly identify the connections between the decisions they made and the organizational results which follow;
3. Accountable leaders do not feel bad for themselves;
4. Instead, accountable leaders take thoughtful, yet swift action to address any and all challenges facing the organization (Hyatt, 2012).

With these truths in mind, school leaders must embrace *total accountability*. They revel in the responsibility their position affords and embrace *total accountability* in two ways: a recognition that leadership is about others and by giving credit away to others.

Effective school leaders are dedicated to the betterment of others. Too often, school leaders ascend to prominent positions only to lead for their own sake. Leadership is not about obtaining a bigger platform or ensuring personal needs are met. In fact, school leadership should be marked by selflessness and servant leadership. As you hope to create a team of selfless individuals, your sole aim must be for the benefit of the collective as well. Williamson (2017) suggested, "A servant leader works tirelessly to develop his or her people and is focused on what they can do for others." In large measure, school leaders should assess their effectiveness based upon the successes of those under their leadership.

School leaders should enthusiastically give credit away to their team. President Harry Truman famously stated, "It is amazing what you can accomplish if you do not care who gets the credit."

In an excellent article on the subject of giving credit away to others, Byron (2018) even remarked, "Sometimes the better approach in a business or work setting is to let others take credit for an idea that you came up with. Similarly, it's gratifying, good for relationships and possibly even for your career to let others share in the credit of your successes." This approach signifies self-assuredness, authentic confidence, and a big-picture mindset. Almost paradoxically, leaders who intentionally give credit to others enjoy increased influence. But, be sure to distribute this credit appropriately, recognizing your employees by the degree of their own impact.

My college basketball coach used to say, "When we win, the credit goes to the players - they played great. When we lose, it is my fault as the coach - I failed us." This was an incredibly prescient comment on leadership. In reality, any number of items could have contributed to a win or loss - foul trouble, injuries, referees, how we shot the basketball, or just plain fortune/misfortune inherent in a sporting event. Still, in the mind of my coach, all those factors paled in comparison to his role and responsibility to the team.

The most effective school leaders adopt a similar mindset. In times of success, they push credit and applause onto others. They eschew adulation, and instead redirect praise to those under their leadership. When outcomes are not positive, they take ownership, reflecting on why the results were not better and devising a plan to ensure the next initiative is more successful.

They are accountable.

# SECTION 2 RESOURCE LIST

Alaimo, K., Olson, C. M., & Frongillo, E. A., Jr. (2001). "Food insufficiency and American children's cognitive, academic and psychosocial development." Pediatrics, 108(3), 824b.

Amabile, T., & Kramer, S. (2011). The progress principle: Using small wins to ignite joy, engagement, and creativity at work. Boston, Mass.: Harvard Business Review Press.

Amen, D. G., & Amen, T. (2017). The brain warrior's way: ignite your energy and focus, attack illness and aging, transform pain into purpose. New York, NY: Berkley.

American Academy of Arts and Sciences. (1873). Horace Mann. Boston and Cambridge, MA.

Bakhtiari, A., Murthi, B., & Steffes, E. (2013). Evaluating the Effect of Affinity Card Programs on Customer Profitability Using Propensity Score Matching. Journal of Interactive Marketing, 27(2), 83–97.

Baumeister, R. F., Bratslavsky, E., Muraven, M., & Tice, D. M. (1998). Ego depletion: Is the active self a limited resource? Journal of Personality and Social Psychology, 74(5), 1252–1265.

Besley, T. and Ghatak, M. (2005) "Competition and Incentives with Motivated Agents", American Economic Review, 95(3): 616-636

*Berrett-Koehler. (2006). Eat that frog!: 21 great ways to stop procrastinating and get more done in less time: 2nd ed. San Francisco, CA.*

*Blanchard, K. (2019). 5 Steps for Servant Leaders to Redirect Behavior. Berrett-Koehler Publishers. Retrieved June 4, 2019.*

*Blanchard, K. (2019). Creating Leadership Ripples. How We Lead. Retrieved June 8, 2019.*

*Books, E. (2015). You are a Badass: How to Stop Doubting Your Greatness and Start Living an Awesome Life. San Francisco: IDreamBooks Inc.*

*Brooks, D. (2011). The social animal: the hidden sources of love, character, and achievement. New York: Random House.*

*Bradberry, T., & Greaves, J. (2009). Emotional intelligence 2.0. San Diego, CA: TalentSmart.*

*Busteed, B., & Auter, Z. (2020, March 13). Why Colleges Should Make Internships a Requirement. Retrieved from https://news.gallup.com/opinion/gallup/222497/why-colleges-internships-requirement.aspx*

*Brown, P. C. (2018). Make It Stick: the science of successful learning. Boston: Bleknap Harvard.*

*Chedid, T. (2018). Depression and anxiety across Parent-child behavior. Psychology and Mental Health Care, 2(4), 01–04. doi: 10.31579/2637-8892/034*

Landy, F. J., & Conte, J. M. (2013). Work in the 21st century: An introduction to industrial and organizational psychology (4th ed.). John Wiley & Sons, Inc..

Conzemius, A. and J. O'Neill. 2002. The Handbook for SMART School Teams. Bloomington, Indiana: National Education Service.

Covey, S. R. (2016). The 7 habits of highly effective people. San Francisco, CA: FranklinCovey Co.

Eisner, E.W. (2003). Arts and the creation of mind. New Haven, CT: Yale University Press.

Eisner, E. (2003). Artistry in education. Scandinavian Journal of Educational Research, 47(3), pp. 373-384. Doi:10.1080/00313830308603. Factors that influence success among racial and ethnic minority college students in the STEM circuit. (2011). ASHE Higher Education Report, 36(6), 53-85.

Expanded Paid Parental Leave Measuring the Impact of Leave on Work & Family, (2019), Boston: Boston College Center for Work & Farmily

Ford, H. (2013). My life and work: Henry fords universal code for world-class success. Portland, or.: Productivity.

Global Talent Trends Study: Mercer (2020). Retrieved from https://www.mercer.com/our-thinking/career/global-talent-hr-trends.html

Goldstein, S. (2017, September 26). EQ Is Massively More Important Than IQ for Leaders. Here's Why. Retrieved from https://www.inc.com/steve-goldstein/eq-is-

*massively-more-important-than-iq-for-leaders-heres-why.html*

Guskey, T. 2000. *Evaluating Professional Development. Thousand Oaks, California: Corwin Press.*

Weiner, B. (2000). *"Intrapersonal and Interpersonal Theories of Motivation from an Attributional Perspective", Educational Psychology Review, 1-14.*

Harnish, V. (2014). *Scaling Up, Ashburn, VA: Gazelle.*

Heath, D., & Heath, C. (2019). *The Power of Moments. Random House UK.*

Job, V., Walton, G. M., Bernecker, K., & Dweck, C. S. (2013). *Beliefs about willpower determine the impact of glucose on self-control. Proceedings of the National Academy of Sciences, 110(37), 14837–14842*

Johnson, S., Cooper, C., Cartwright, S., Doland, I., Taylor, P. and Millet, C. (2005) *"The experience of work-related stress across occupations", Journal of Managerial Psychology, 20, 2: 178-187*

Kambouris, A. (2018). *How Humility Keeps Your Ego From Hijacking Your Leadership and Team Success. Entrepreneur. Retrieved May 28, 2019.*

Keller, G., & Papasan, J. (2017). *The one thing: the surprisingly simple truth behind extraordinary results. Austin, TX: Bard Press.*

Kleinman, R. E., Murphy, J. M., Little, M., Pagano, M., Wehler, C. A., Regal, K., & Jellinek, M. S. (1998). *Hunger in children in the United States: Potential behavioral and emotional correlates. Pediatrics,*

*101(1), E3. Retrieved from:*
*http://pediatrics.aappublications.org/content/101/1/e3.l*
*ong*

*Klein, G. (2014, August 1). Performing a Project Premortem.*
*Retrieved from https://hbr.org/2007/09/performing-a-*
*project-premortem*

*Klein, J. (2004). Planning middle school schedules for*
*improved attention and achievement. Scandinavian*
*Journal of Educational Research, 48(4), 441-450.*

*Kohll, A. (2018, July 11). What Employees Really Want At*
*Work. Retrieved from*
*https://www.forbes.com/sites/alankohll/2018/07/10/wha*
*t-employees-really-want-at-work/#7c71b4945ad3*

*Kruse, K. (2015) 15 Secrets Successful People Know about*
*Time Management: The Productivity Habits of 7*
*Billionaires, 13 Olympic Athletes, 29 Straight-A*
*Students, and 239 Entrepreneurs, 1st edn. Philadelphia,*
*PA: The Kruse Group.*

*Learning How to Learn: Powerful mental tools to help you*
*master tough subjects. (n.d.). Retrieved from*
*https://www.coursera.org/learn/learning-how-to-learn*

*Lencioni, P. (2004). Death by meeting: a leadership fable*
*about solving the most painful problem in business. San*
*Francisco: Wiley.*

*Liu, A. G., Ford, N. A., Hu, F. B., Zelman, K. M.,*
*Mozaffarian, D., & Kris-Etherton, P. M. (2017). A*
*healthy approach to dietary fats: understanding the*
*science and taking action to reduce consumer*
*confusion. Nutrition journal, 16(1), 53.*

*https://doi.org/10.1186/s12937-017-0271-4*

Maslach, C., Jackson, S. E., & Leiter, M. P. (2018). Maslach burnout inventory: manual. Menlo Park, CA: Mind Garden.

Mead, N. L., Alquist, J. L., & Baumeister, R. F. (2010). Ego Depletion and the Limited Resource Model of Self-Control. Self Control in Society, Mind, and Brain, 375–388. doi: 10.1093/acprof:oso/9780195391381.003.0020

Meer, H. V. D., & Buijs, J. (2012). The Progress Principle - By Teresa Amabile and Steven Kramer. Creativity and Innovation Management, 21(2), 242–243. doi: 10.1111/j.1467-8691.2012.00645.x

Millar, K., Styles, B., & Wastell, D. (1980). Time of day and retrieval from long term memory. British Journal of Psychology, 71, 407-414.

Newport, C. (2018). Deep Work: rules for focused success in a distracted world. New York, NY: Grand Central Publishing.

Oakley, B. (2018). Learning How to Learn: How to Succeed in School Without Spending All Your Time Studying; a Guide for Kids and Teens. London: Penguin Publishing Group.

Oppezzo, M., & Schwartz, D. L. (2014). Give your ideas some legs: The positive effect of walking on creative thinking. Journal of Experimental Psychology: Learning, Memory, and Cognition, 40(4), 1142–1152.

Osterwalder, A., & Pigneur, Y. (2010). Business model generation: a handbook for visionaries, game changers, and challengers. Hoboken, NJ: Wiley.

*Pang, A. S.-K. (2017). Rest: Why you get more done when you work less. London: Penguin Life.*

*Pekrun, R., Goetz, T., Daniels, L. M., Stupnisky, R. H., & Perry, R. P. (2010). Boredom in achievement settings: Exploring control-value antecedents and performance outcomes of a neglected emotion. Journal of Educational Psychology, 102, 531–549.*

*Pintrich, P. R., & Garcia, T. (1991). Student goal orientation and self-regulation in the college classroom. In M. L. Maehr, & P. R. Pintrich, Advances in motivation and achievement (Vol 7). Goals and selfregulatory processes (pp. 371–402). Greenwich, CT: JAI Press.*

*Ripplematch, (2020). Will Gen Z be the Next Generation of Job Hoppers? (n.d.). Retrieved from https://ripplematch.com/journal/article/will-gen-z-be-the-next-generation-of-job-hoppers-b04feb4e/*

*Rose, J. (2012, May 9). How to Break Free of Our 19th-Century Factory-Model Education System. Retrieved from https://www.theatlantic.com/business/archive/2012/05/how-to-break-free-of-our-19th-century-factory-model-education-system/256881/*

*Russell, B., & Steinberg, A. (2010). Red and me: my coach, my lifelong friend. New York: Harper, p. 9.*

*Tett, G. (2013, April 19). Interview: Facebook's Sheryl Sandberg. Retrieved from https://www.ft.com/content/da931d58-a7c2-11e2-9fbe-00144feabdc0*

Tracy, B. (2016). *Eat that frog!: get more of the important things done - today! London: Hodder & Stoughton.*

Visram, T. (2019, June 3). *Why aren't more workers taking parental leave? Retrieved from https://www.fastcompany.com/90358199/why-arent-more-workers-taking-parental-leave?partner=rss&utm_source=twitter.com&utm_me dium=social&utm_campaign=rss+fastcompany&utm_content=rss*

Wickman, G. (2012). *Traction. Dallas: Benbella Books.*

# Section 3: Continual Evaluation

*"This is the power of the flywheel. Success breeds support and commitment, which breeds even greater success, which breeds more support and commitment, round and around the flywheel goes." - Jim Collins (Good to Great And The Social Sectors, p. 24)*

The continual evaluation is a repeating process that helps evaluate and assess school needs and ensures a systematic continuation of school culture fit. This stage is called the *Continuous Evaluation Stage* and is conducted after the Discovery Stage is completed. We have adopted a school flywheel (Collins, 2019) to illustrate the Continuous Evaluation Stage below. With this in mind, schools may adapt the flywheel to meet their own unique context.

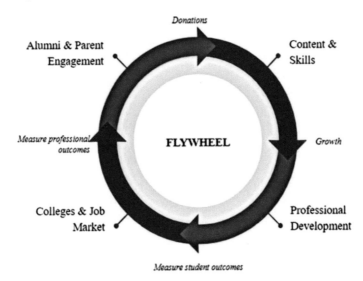

# CONTENT AND SKILLS

The graph above showcases various stages that the school flywheel signifies. As discussed above, each school will develop its own flywheel to determine what is most important to them as an institution.

Content and skills are the core of the student's learning experience in the classroom. Schools need to continually assess if the content and skills they are offering are followed with successful outcomes for their students. The "content and skills" element contains similarities to a scope and sequence or curricular map. Yet, there are a few key distinctions of the "content and skills" element of the flywheel.

First, the Flywheel utilizes a process-based approach. It outlines the core skills students will acquire. The Flywheel also identifies the content knowledge a graduate of a school will possess. Additionally, it deciphers what tools the school has equipped students with so that they are able to pursue knowledge and skill development. Therefore, the second distinction is that content and skills are fluid and ongoing, meaning that they do not end at the conclusion of a particular marking period. The learning of content and skill represent a process that continues well beyond graduation. Finally, content and skills allows for personalization on the part of students. As students approach graduation, they should have a degree of autonomy in identifying the skills and knowledge that will most critically serve them in the years to come.

Today, there is much debate surrounding the ratio of skills versus content that ought to be taught in schools (Kettler, 2019). Skills are about adaptability. These two very different sets of learning goals–content and skills– require different teaching and learning strategies to facilitate their acquisition. Some educational institutions have even replaced their assessments with a skill-based curriculum that is reflected in a new type of transcript called the Mastery Transcript. Regardless of the decision a school makes regarding the ratio, school leaders must continually evaluate the degree to which the learning students engage in directly prepares them to succeed beyond the walls of the school.

# GROWTH

The growth of a student plays an immense role when evaluating the effectiveness of the school environment. Student growth should be expected across the entire student experience - academic, social/emotional, arts, athletics, service, and self-confidence. Typically, academic growth itself is a measurable unit that is usually assessed at the end of a marking period. This snapshot in time is too limited and does not show the "bigger" picture. Such an approach is simply unable to measure trends, pace, and patterns of growth and learning which takes place on a daily, weekly, and monthly basis.

Instead, daily progress of a student should be the main focus. Teresa Amabile and Steven Kramer discovered that small achievements spur motivation and growth (Amabile & Kramer, 2012). Celebrating 'micro-wins' allows students to receive real-time feedback. For a student who is currently struggling in any way, this small victory allows for a more grand success to be achieved. Instead of looking at the grade that will take months to improve, the student has the ability to approach "today" as a tangible opportunity for excellence, accentuating the positive during this process.

The idea of continual, daily growth certainly is integral to understanding how to improve a student's performance in the classroom. Therefore, this type of growth needs to be measured. This growth, however, should shift from the daily checking of grades and into reflection. Specifically, how have I improved today as a student?

Schools should also move away from the model of competition amongst students and encourage an individual competition of a student with himself or herself. The question students should be asking themselves is, "How was my today compared to my yesterday?" Such an approach will stimulate progress, even if it accounts for just 1% a week. This tactic of self-improvement and personal achievement aligns with the type of smaller, measurable key results discussed previously.

# PROFESSIONAL DEVELOPMENT

We previously discussed professional development in connection with the staff experience. Here, we extend the discussion to underscore its importance and apply the topic directly to the school's academic program. As school leaders think about the flywheel, professional development is critical to ensure that staff members not only grow, but develop skills and competencies that align with their school's instructional program.

For example, a school emphasizing a blended-learning instructional model must ensure their teachers' professional development program addresses the specific instructional technologies the school utilizes. In truth, professional development can only be tackled after school leaders obtain a thorough understanding of the content and skills the school aspires to teach students. Thus, a school's proficiency relative to curriculum mapping and vertically integrating subject areas across grade-levels and divisions becomes critical to the efficacy of its professional development. In fact, "...To ensure a coherent system that supports teachers across the entire professional continuum, professional learning should link to their experiences in preparation and induction, as well as to teaching standards and evaluation" (Effective Teacher Professional Learning, 2017).

This process channels the approach to learning and development made famous by legendary thinker, Stephen Covey: "begin with the end in mind" (Covey, 1989). Once achieved, school leaders can implement a professional development program that supports teachers in providing content and skills in fresh, effective, and engaging ways for students. As school leaders seek school culture fit, a meaningful and targeted investment in professional development remains a critical priority.

# MEASURE STUDENT OUTCOMES

For independent schools, it is imperative to match the stakeholders' jobs-to-be-done with their realized outcomes. For example, if the jobs-to-be-done for parents is to have college acceptances at elite schools, such an outcome must be measured by the school.

Methodologies that are used to measure student learning each have their own limitations and biases, and no method can be counted on to be completely error free. That is why best practice in educational research dictates triangulating the data. If several different sources of data are used, it increases the probability that the findings present an accurate picture (NHSC, 2012). In other words, the strongest assessment programs will rely on a mix of direct and indirect measures to determine if you are solving the jobs-to-be-done.

One way to collect data is through both indirect and direct measures. At the college and university level, indirect measures include data from surveys of seniors and alumni, retention rates, graduation rates, number of students progressing to advanced degrees, etc. They allow school leaders, faculty, researchers, and consumers to infer the benefits to students from their years in college, but they cannot report with precision exactly what students have learned or what they are capable of doing as a result of their university education. Historically, these kinds of data have been collected by offices of institutional research, alumni offices, etc.

Direct measures provide more evidence of the increase in students' knowledge and abilities over a period of time. Standardized tests as, for example, the Collegiate Learning Assessment (CLA) are one kind of direct measure. While the CLA assesses general education skills, other standardized tests can measure specific disciplinary knowledge. The Force Concept Inventory, for instance, is used to determine students' understanding of concepts in mechanics." (MIT.edu, 2017). Private and independent schools at the secondary level may choose to identify their own benchmarks.

# COLLEGE AND JOB MARKET

The ultimate measure regarding how well schools serve their students are the results measured after graduation. Do your students succeed in college and in the job market? Do they become successful members of society and how does your school define 'success'? Are your students enthusiastically promoting your school? Do they confirm that their training at your school strongly sets them on a path of achievement and significance? Obtaining college and job market information is important because it will help in your assessment of your content and skills. The National High School Center organizes the college and career readiness outcomes and measures by scanning organizations involved in college and career readiness. Among the most common academic/technical performance and engagement measures are coursework and assessment scores.

In addition to coursework, more states are administering end-of-course assessments to increase rigor and facilitate better alignment between state standards and curriculum as well as additional testing to track students' college and career readiness (ACT, 2011). Beyond academic measures, some districts and high schools are also measuring students' social and emotional learning and engagement with schooling in recognition of the importance of these factors to success after high school. Therefore, we look to measure outcomes beyond school such as professional outcomes and donations back to the school from alumni.

# MEASURE PROFESSIONAL OUTCOMES

We discussed previously the importance of setting outcomes and then subdividing into measurable milestones to track progress. The same approach is applied at measuring the professional progress of students. The question you should ask yourself is what are the key goals schools envisions for its alumni?[4]

---

[4] Key results have traditionally been called key performance indicators, or "KPIs". For list of examples of KPIs *See* https://www.scoro.com/blog/key-performance-indicators-examples/

*School Culture Fit*

# ALUMNI AND PARENT ENGAGEMENT

Engaging the extended community of your school is integral to keeping school culture fit strong and sustainable. There are multiple ways to achieve such a strong bond. And, as we see with many schools, it's not as easy as it may appear at first glance.

Consider an example from the University of Michigan. Although the university enjoys outstanding school spirit and a large alumni base, over time, alumni enthusiasm and engagement plateaued. Beginning in 2007, fundraising had become a growing issue. The student calling center did not invest in promoting an organizational morale, unable to facilitate alumni gifts. The university took measures immediately, contacting Adam Grant, a Wharton professor and organizational psychologist. He initiated a process of ingraining morale within employees at the center, resulting in an increased alumni giving.

Grant decided that those who received financial aid in the past should talk to the students in the call center. Hence, the students had an opportunity to see how financial donations impacted the lives of their recipients. They also could share those powerful stories with the alumni base. What Grant focused on was making sure to eloquently illustrate the values historically ingrained within the University of Michigan and strategically pass these objectives over to the next generation of students. That way, alumni could see their impact and were empowered to engage in meaningful work that was greatly appreciated.

The outcomes of the new program were phenomenal. Student engagement increased to by 142% as they spent more time talking with alumni and making meaningful connections. This increased engagement translated into an increase of 172% in donations. What Grant achieved was a new model of connecting bridges by attaching certain meaning to each individual giving. The call center was no longer perceived as a money-making machine, but rather an enriching opportunity to give back to their alma mater.

In 2014, Bullis School (MD) opted to use the power of meaning as the framework for its entrepreneurship program. The goal was to build students' life skills—growth mindset, grit, and resilience—while teaching them about entrepreneurship at its core. To better serve the students, the program was designed to effectively utilize the experience and expertise of both alumni and parents.

This two-part framework, individual meaning of a student and parent/alumni engagement, not only fostered community building, but also stimulated philanthropic activity within the school.

# PROMOTING STUDENT MEANING

The program we designed was aimed at creating a collaborative and intellectually-challenging environment. In the program, students are split in five teams, tasked to design their own concept and implement the prototype to enhance the user experience. The program ends in a Shark Tank-style pitch competition where the winning team receives $10,000 to pursue its business idea after graduation. The 2019 winner, Rockabyebackpack, a diaper bag that converts into a changing station, has recently gained over $4,000 in shipments of the product.

In college, alumni raise investments and get initial customer segments in years ahead. For example, Vana Learning, a tutoring and coaching software, won Vanderbilt Center for Teaching's Do Good award, and Kanga Trash Solutions, a clean, modern collection bag for large venues, won grants at the University of Maryland.

Students pursued their business initiatives because the program was not a typical classroom setting, but rather an immersive entrepreneurial accelerator. Former students find the program especially useful when they are deciding which majors to pursue and what skills to prioritize during their college years.

Lastly, the program is designed to help students overcome fears of failure. In today's educational setting, performance assessment is based on the successful end-result, not the process. Such limited evaluation disables students to experiment and foster their imagination. Since the program is process-oriented, the teams are primed to experiment and learn from mistakes, which improves student's self-esteem. Transforming assessment tools and focusing on the path, not the outcome, makes a direct impact on a student's performance post-graduation.

Co-author, Marc Steren, designed the Entrepreneurship program described above. Six months prior to his start date, Marc designed the concept that would focus on content knowledge and skills. An extensive business experience and months of interviews with entrepreneurs, parents, alumni, helped him to identify the holes within the current system. The results were extraordinary, by pulling alumni/parents into the program, the schools achieved a significantly greater level of engagement which in turn led to better outcomes, such as better learning and more donations.

There are many opportunities to learn from parents about what they want to achieve for their child's education. Understanding what "outcomes" are important for their children helps teachers to align classes accordingly. Obtaining this knowledge often starts by simply asking for parent feedback.

In leveraging parent expertise for student learning, teachers must ensure that parent presenters "fit" at the right time, giving a lesson that matches the students' concepts. In this way, guest speakers provide relevant and applicable insight. Teachers are better equipped to design student-centric curriculum maps.

Yearly, more parents and alumni are stepping forward to offer mentorship for students. Turning down volunteers is the last thing you should do, but ensuring that the "value" is attached to each offer is a massive undertaking. In case there is excess supply of mentors, you should consider designing speaker series, coffee chats, office hours or any other engagement platforms to establish bridges with students and parent experts.

Alumni engagement also fosters entrepreneurial programs at your school. A great example is the BUzz Lab seen below, which is overly reliant on the personal relationships of the BUzz Lab faculty and in need of relationship management support. They reach a large and diverse student and alumni audience of approximately 4,000. BUzz Lab faculty maintain deep ties with diverse members of the entrepreneurial ecosystem.

Based on the MIT Case, we suggest utilizing the framework "Stimulate, Educate, Incubate" to create the entrepreneurial university at your school (Elia et al., 2017).

| Entrepreneurial School | | |
| --- | --- | --- |
| **Stimulate** | **Educate** | **Incubate** |
| S1. Supportive Staff & Faculty<br>S2. Success Stories and Role Models<br>S3. Introductory Courses | E1. Form a Team<br>E2. Validate Idea<br>E3. Pitch the Idea<br>E4. Develop a business plan and a prototype | I1. Mentoring<br>I2. Networking<br>I3. Business model competitions<br>I4. Funding |

In addition to sharing their expertise with students, the volunteers feel like active participants of the school community, and they truly are. For example, one attorney helps students incorporate their businesses, while another attorney works with students on defining and securing their intellectual property. Parents and alumni can share their expertise in negotiations, building sales funnels, scaling, SEO, educational marketing, diversity, venture capital, and more. They also offer internships to students. These conversations and networking allows students to venture on their own, as it happened with a former student of the programm, who designed "Student Internship Network," helping to connect students with potential internships offered by alumni and parents.

# DONATIONS

Sharing their experience with students, alumni and parents grow even more fond of the institution and subsequently, are more inclined to financially support your programs at the school. Listed below are successful stories of meaningful and engaging integration.

One parent-mentor was an active member of the Young Professional Organization (YPO), a renowned global organization that helps chief executives learn and grow. He was beyond impressed with the program, particularly with the impact he could make through his contribution. Enjoying the program, he soon reached out to find more ways to contribute. His eagerness to help turned into a schools-wide YPO event that later brought large personal donations. The mentor himself officially joined the board by taking a role of student recruiter. His motivations were clear - he wanted to help not only because he was a parent, but most importantly because of his active involvement which primed strong dedication to the school community. Sociological theories posit that people give in expectation of reciprocation or are influenced by modeling, social pressures and reinforcement, and desire for status (Hatfield, Walster, and Piliavin, 1978). By tapping into these motives, you can expand your donor base.

Another parent, who was inspired by how others were engaging with the program, reached out to the program coordinator to find ways he could be helpful himself. As an experienced entrepreneur, he knew that a lack of initial funding can keep even the best business ideas from getting off the ground. He agreed to underwrite the "shark tank" award for 10 consecutive years (a $100,000 gift) and gave the school an additional $10,000 gift for general purposes.

Finally, others gave the school keystone gifts of $5 million dollars each to help fund the Discovery Center, a 70,000-square-foot building on the Bullis campus for STEM, entrepreneurship, and the arts that we announced we would build at the inception of the entrepreneurship program. Because their children participated in the program, the parents had a direct insight on the importance of entrepreneurship. Beyond the entrepreneurship program, you should keep focusing on expanding the reach of our alumni and parent outreach. Ultimately, you will build a highly comprehensive ecosystem where parents and alumni add true value—both programmatically and financially—to the student body. The first step is to ensure that you are offering *meaningful* participation to all people involved.

*Note: the principles of the case study above can be applied to any academic program. The idea is to leverage the expertise, resources, and enthusiasm of the greater school community to improve student learning and institutional outcomes.

# SECTION 3 REFERENCE LIST

*Amabile, T & Kramer, S. (2011). The Progress Principle: Using Small Wins to Ignite Joy, Engagement and Creativity at Work, Boston, MA, Harvard Business School Publishing*

*Baldoni, J. (2010). Vision, Mission, and Values: Yes, They Still Matter.* **Fast Company.** *Retrieved June 22, 2019.*

*Bergdahl, M. (2018). Putting Your Employees First: The ABCs for Leaders of Generations X, Y, & Z.*

*Byron, P. (2018). How Giving Credit to Others at Work Helps You Develop the Habit of Giving. medium.com. Retrieved on January 30, 2019.*

*Calipari, J. (2016). Success Is The Only Option: The Art of Coaching Extreme Talent. New York, NY: HarperCollins.*

*Cathy, S. T. (2002). Eat Mor Chikin, Inspire More People: Doing Business the Chick-Fil-A Way. Decatur, GA: Looking Glass Books.*

*Collins, J. (2001) Good to Great: Why Some Companies Make the Leap and Others Don't, New York, NY. HarpersCollins Publishing*

*Collins, J. (2005). Good to Great And The Social Sectors: A Monograph to Accompany Good to Great.*

*Collins, J. (2019) Turning the Flywheel: Why Some Companies Build Momentum and Others Don't. New York., NY. HarpersCollins Publishing.*

Covey, S. (1989). *The 7 Habits of Highly Effective People.* New York, NY: Free Press.

Eastman, K. (2019). *Time Zones: Spare Time. Part Time. Full Time. kevineastman.net.* Retrieved May 5, 2019.

Ebben, J. (2005). *Developing Effective Mission and Vision Statements. Inc.* Retrieved June 22, 2019.

*Effective Teacher Professional Learning.* (2017). *Designing and Implementing Effective Professional Learning,* 9–18.

Elia, G., Secundo, G., & Passiante, G. (2017). *Pathways towards the entrepreneurial university for creating entrepreneurial engineers: an Italian case. International Journal of Entrepreneurship and Innovation Management, 21(1/2),* 27. doi: 10.1504/ijeim.2017.081486

Gheen, M., Smerdon, B., Hein, V., & Lebow, M. (2012). *Outcomes and measures of college and career success: How do we know when high school graduates meet expectations?* Washington, DC: National High School Center

Kettler, R. J. (2019). *School Psychology and the Scientific Method. Research Methodologies of School Psychology,* 3–23. doi: 10.4324/9781315724072-1

Koma, A. (2016). *Buzz Williams Leads His "Get Better Group" To Help Build Culture, Character. TheKeyPlay.* Retrieved May 25, 2019.

Knight, R. (1991). *A Proposed Approach to Teaching Entrepreneurship. Journal of Small Business and Entrepreneurship.*

Kruse, K. (2013). *What Is Leadership? Forbes.* Retrieved May 21, 2019.

Newport, C. (2018). *Deep Work: rules for focused success in a distracted world. New York: Grand Central Publishing.*

Walster, E., Walster, G. W., & Traupmann, J. (1978). *Equity and premarital sex. Journal of Personality and Social Psychology, 36(1), 82–92.*

# Section 4: 12 Traits of Thriving School Cultures

"Organizational Culture is the "water" in the fishbowl. If the water is clean, nourishing, energizing the fish will thrive and if the water is toxic the fish will die, leaving the infrastructure valueless." - Ranjan De Silva

Schools must not be satisfied in simply achieving school culture fit. Indeed, they must preserve it. We will now explore 12 traits that are integral to ensuring the preservation and sustaining of school culture fit. Fortunately, these enduring principles are accessible and available to every school and every school leader.

Here is a checkbox of the twelve traits:

1. Cultivate Motivated Employees
2. Make the Little Things a Big Deal
3. Validate Ambition and Hire the Best
4. Make Recognition of Others a Habit
5. Hire For Culture Fit
6. Cultivate a Selfless Team Culture
7. Promote From Within
8. Lead With Open Eyes and Full Hearts
9. Make Strategic Planning a Habit
10. Commit to Ensuring Equity for All Community Members
11. Employ a Shared Leadership Model
12. Embrace Change

# CULTIVATE MOTIVATED EMPLOYEES

*"Motivation is the fuel, necessary to keep the human engine running." - Zig Ziglar*

*Matt's story*

After high school, I attended a military preparatory school for a postgraduate year. My focus was to further improve as a basketball player, and the postgraduate year had become a relatively popular path for players who wanted to capture an extra year for development. This extra year allowed for more time for strength training and also provided a year of outstanding competition versus other top postgraduate teams and excellent junior college programs. The best part was the postgraduate year did not count towards the four years of collegiate eligibility. From an athletic perspective, it was a free year.

It was also a military environment. We wore Battle Dress Uniforms every day, and lived on a military base. We took college-level courses and received military training. Our daily schedule began very early, finishing with 'study barracks' until 10:00pm. There were some tough days. Still, one of my teammates, Nicky, will forever serve as an example of elite motivation.

Nicky possessed an indomitable spirit. He seemed to bring a relentless energy to everything he did. At 6:00am Physical Training formations, Nicky was smiling and barking encouragement to his peers. In the middle of a grueling basketball practice, Nicky never stopped pushing us with his positive energy. On weekends before a big exam, when the rest of us were frustrated that we had to stay in to study, Nicky would remind us of our purpose and help us see the big picture by setting the example through his 'happy warrior' approach to his courses.

Simply stated, Nicky was the most motivated teammate I have ever known. My only regret is that I didn't seek to understand his motivation. I should have inquired as to where his boundless energy, optimistic outlook, and belief came from. It would be tremendously valuable to me today.

Still, as I look back on the value Nicky provided to our team, on and off the court, it was immeasurable. Nicky was a good player on a very talented team. Although he rarely played in games, he was our engine. Nicky set forth a standard. And the rest of us felt an obligation to operate on his level, to lift our efforts on days when we otherwise felt tired or discouraged.

The lesson I take from Nicky's example and his impact on our team is how important motivated team members are. At one point in the season, a national publication ranked our basketball team the 8th best postgraduate team in the United States. I believe we could have achieved much more. What if each player shared Nicky's motivation? What if our entire team approached life with the type of engagement that Nicky modeled? Truly, the sky would have been the limit.

As school leaders seek to sustain school culture fit, it is critical that they cultivate motivation across the staff. We may not all be Nicky, yet school leaders can intentionally create conditions facilitative of motivated and inspired staff members. Through recent research in Organizational Behavior, we know that employees need a system that values association, growth, and an environment that is both supportive and mitigates negative factors[5] (McCelland, 1961). A motivated employee, therefore, is one that:

- Has attainable, yet challenging goals;
- Understands the culture fit of the school;
- Has potential for growth;
- Enjoys an emotionally safe community;
- And engages in an intellectually-thriving environment (reWork, 2019).[6]

---

[5] *See also*, Willpower Doesn't Work stating that the surrounding environment is more important than intrinsic motivation.

[6] *See* Google's Project Aristotle.

In cultivating motivated employees, school leaders must build an organization that provides both extrinsic and intrinsic motivation. Intrinsic motivation looks at the job itself. Consider the following 7 reflection questions:

- Is the job challenging enough?
- Do I have autonomy to make decisions?
- Do I clearly see a connection between my role and the mission and vision of the school?
- Does what I do matter?
- Am I positively impacting others in a tangible way?
- Am I growing?
- Does my current role tap into my strengths and areas of giftedness?

Such questions address the intrinsic motivation of staff members. On the other hand, extrinsic motivation refers to the rewards that are achievable from the organization such as increased pay, and as we discussed previously, recognition (Lepper, et al., 1973). Explained further, "Extrinsic motivation is any reason we do the work other than the joy of doing the work itself. Anything that we are promised for doing the work or anything that we get as a result of doing the work are all extrinsic motivators" (Burkus, 2020). Extrinsic motivation is transactional. Consider the illustration below:

| Action | Outcome | Reward |
|--------|---------|--------|

Often, the action is performed not only with the goal of achieving a specific outcome, but with the express expectation of the specific reward in mind.

Hackman and Oldman (1976) developed a job satisfaction scale that looks at both intrinsic and extrinsic factors (Conte & Landy p. 344):

- Skill variety- The number of skills required to perform a task. - Intrinsic;

- Ask Identity- Is the job self-contained with a clear beginning, middle and end? - Intrinsic;
- Task Significance- Is the task important to the organization, even if that importance is merely perceived? - Extrinsic.
- Autonomy- Do teachers, within your school's framework, have the opportunity to make meaningful decisions? - Intrinsic.
- Feedback- Do teachers receive consistent feedback and recognition for a job well done? - Extrinsic.

As a school leader, you must pursue talented staff members. In addition, you must ensure that your school culture aligns with an employee-centric working environment where your colleagues can thrive and grow together with the organization. There is a common misbelief that employee performance and satisfaction are proportional to the size of one's paycheck. While compensation matters, it is not determinative in creating motivated employees. School leaders must carefully nurture their school culture to facilitate a motivated staff.

What could your school achieve if your team increased, and sustained, their level of motivation?

# MAKE THE LITTLE THINGS A BIG DEAL

*"Handle the little things well; for they
become the great things." - Flo Falayi*

*Matt's story*

What seems like a *little thing* to one person, can be a *big deal* to someone else.

This is most certainly true for school leaders. I remember my first year as a teacher as if it happened just yesterday. To people around me, I was a confident, enthusiastic 24 year-old, with more ideas and opinions than I knew what to do with. Internally, however, I was nervous and desperately seeking the approval of my principal and colleagues.

One afternoon my principal, Dr. Ben Phillips, walked into my classroom in the middle of a lecture. This was an unannounced visit. For Dr. Phillips, this visit was likely one of several he would engage in that day. And relative to the other activities on his agenda that day, this visit was likely of low consequence.

For me, the classroom visit was a different story altogether. Upon my boss entering the classroom and taking up residence in an empty seat in the back of the room, I found myself experiencing all the signs of nervous energy - if not even anxiety. This reaction had nothing to do with my principal's character or previous behavior. In fact, my reaction to his visit was contrary to his character. Dr. Phillips was as kind and caring as any person you could meet. I was reacting to a desire for his approval. And I wasn't sure if I measured up to his standards.

As it relates to the lesson, I was lecturing on a critical world event, focusing on the geography of a certain battle by scaling the locations down to local towns in our region of the state. I believe the illustration was creative and facilitated student learning. Dr. Phillips did as well.

153

In fact, he left me a short note, handwritten, that complimented my illustration and affirmed the work I was doing in the classroom. I kept that note in my desk drawer for two years. I reread it periodically as an encouragement. At times of doubt, it served as a reminder of validation and approval that would quiet the imposter syndrome that can be deafening for any first year teacher.

Looking back, there was a lot of constructive feedback that Dr. Phillips could have written to me that day. There were countless ways I could have improved the lesson. And undoubtedly, Dr. Phillips could have rattled them off in his note to me. He also could have simply left the classroom. He was certainly busy. Perhaps, a casual affirmation as we passed in the hallway over the next couple of days would have sufficed as a follow up.

Yet, he did not use that classroom visit as a coaching session. And, he did take the time to write me a personal note. Upon reflection, I believe he knew, consistent with the strong instructional leader that he is, how important this classroom visit was to me. He knew that what I needed that day was a personal sign of encouragement and validation. The instructional coaching could wait.

Dr. Phillips also knew how significant a handwritten note would be for me. He knew I needed the affirmation, from my supervisor, that he saw my efforts and approved of my work.

I have never forgotten it. And I am grateful for his simple act that was so pivotal to my connection with the school. In the scope of his day, it was a *little thing*. Yet for me, it was most certainly a *big deal*.

Strategic school leaders recognize that small actions, gestures, and seemingly innocuous behaviors create a powerful, cumulative impact (MacDonald, 2000, p. 26). They model 'giver' behaviors. Examples of these 'small things' include:

- Writing an affirming note;
- Fixing the jammed copier;
- Putting on another pot of coffee;
- Unlocking team member's doors and turning their classroom or office lights on in the morning before they arrive;

- Active listening;
- Smiling;
- Sending kind and respectful emails;
- Holding doors;
- Reloading the copier with printer paper;
- Cleaning the staff room fridge;
- Replacing the empty Kleenex box.

And the list most certainly goes on.

School leaders should not necessarily attend to every item on the list every day. The point is to be mindful of opportunities to serve and contribute to the well-being of others. The more influential your position of leadership, the more powerful such acts of selflessness become.

Effective school leaders also celebrate team members who habitually demonstrate these actions. They make a *big deal* out of these *little things*. Why? Because these actions are not insignificant at all. Cumulatively, repeated day in and day out, they contribute to a positive school culture. They beautifully represent the traits of a thriving community in which any contribution is perceived as equally important and meaningful. When the culture reflects a selfishness, lack of care for others, and a lack of collective responsibility, low morale almost certainly looms nearby. Conversely, when selflessness, respect, and humility flourish, positive morale arises and persists.

In their best-selling book *The Go-Giver: A Little Story About a Powerful Business Idea,* Bob Burg and John David Mann outlined for individuals 5 Laws of Stratospheric Success. The laws are outlined below:

| The Law of Value | Underscores the importance of giving more than you take. |
|---|---|
| The Law of Compensation | Emphasizes that your income (or success) is directly proportional to the degree to which you serve others. |
| The Law of Influence | States that your influence grows only when you genuinely put the interests of your peers ahead of your own. |
| The Law of Authenticity | Reminds us that we are enough, just as we are. In fact, the more we act in alignment to who we truly are, the more effective we will be. |
| The Law of Receptivity | Implores us to receive generosity from others. |

Each of these 5 Laws of Stratospheric Success urge leaders to give, serve, act selflessly, operate with authentic humility and without pretense, and to be emotionally open and available to colleagues. And yet these are rarely natural behaviors. Even with the best intentions at heart, school leaders often fail to exemplify these behaviors personally and celebrate them publicly. They may simply feel too busy. Perhaps the demands of the job create an emotional bankruptcy. In either event, it can be difficult to carve out the time or emotional energy throughout the school day to be fully present among students, staff, and families.

And yet, those 10 minutes at the carpool line, waving and smiling at parents and students as they leave campus for the day, create significant goodwill and facilitate the 'giver' culture. Sitting down with staff during lunch can open up pathways for establishing meaningful and trusted relationships with your employees. Investing only five minutes to clean out the refrigerator in the staff lounges represents the power of servant leadership across campus. Not to mention that you will serve as an example for your staff and students, which will foster the "giver" culture across the entire school community.

Countless other examples of 'making the little things a big deal' most certainly exist. As a school leader, you have an incredible opportunity to simply model these behaviors as part of your school's standard operating procedure. And once you do, the giving culture will prevail.

# VALIDATE AMBITION AND HIRE THE BEST

*"The starting point of all achievement is desire." - Napoleon Hill*

When we talk about ambition, we often refer to organizational citizenship behavior, which deals with the actions and behaviors that are not required by workers. They are not critical to the job, but benefit the team and encourage even greater organizational functioning and efficiency.

This is typically categorized as a worker "going above and beyond," or "giving their all." They look at their job as more than just a paycheck and strive to do all they can to make their work environment run smoothly; even if it has a minimal connection to their current duties.

Oftentimes, ambition is seen to be a detrimental quality. The word *ambition* can be associated with selfishness, greed, or manipulation. Yet, professional ambition is not a negative personal characteristic. Instead, ambition should be leveraged to further the development of your school culture. Ambitious team members should never be seen as a broken wheel, but rather as a resource for mutual growth and improvement.

In his 2017 book, *Vivid Vision: A Remarkable Tool For Aligning Your Business Around a Shared Vision of the Future*, Cameron Herold outlined the extraordinary benefits leaders enjoy by establishing a compelling, 'vivid vision' of the future (Herold, 2017). Creating a picture of what their desired future looks like three years henceforth, Herold implored leaders to be ambitious. He cited the term, "BHAG" (Big Hairy Audacious Goals) to represent the scope leaders should embrace when creating their 'vivid vision' (Collins & Porras, 1994). As organizations aim to achieve BHAG's, they will need ambitious team members who are both talented and industrious. Consequently, school leaders must nurture the ambition of their team members. They must have staff members who are excellent in their roles and who have an eye towards a bigger future.

As a school leader, you should not simply create your own vivid vision for the school you lead. Instead, you should empower and encourage leaders across the school community to create a vivid vision for the departments, programs, grade-levels, and divisions they lead. In doing so, you will unleash tremendous creativity and energy across campus. Provided such visions are complementary to, and in alignment with, the school's collective vivid vision, these localized visions serve to further engage staff in their front-line work. And if these efforts are to prove fruitful, you will need ambitious staff members willing to take on BHAG's across the school community.

Indeed, schools need ambitious teachers and school leaders. Ambitious educators pursue creative endeavors, push the envelope, challenge the status quo, and take on both intellectual and professional challenges. Ultimately, as the ambitious team members set higher standards and expectations, the overall team performance will improve and other members will be more motivated to go the extra mile. Synergy can exist between personal ambition and team success. You need to recognize that personal goals and organizational objectives do not have to be separate and distinct. In reality, personal ambition can and should be validated and then aligned with the objectives of the school. When it is not, ambitious team members often become disgruntled and formulate an agenda separate from that of the school.

School leaders should embrace this reality, being mindful of what each team member's personal ambitions are, while identifying ways to help them grow through mentoring and the provision of strategic growth opportunities. Soon, a more positive culture will be cultivated.

As a school leader, consider the following questions:
- Do you know the goals and ambitions of your team members?
- How are you supporting their career ambitions through the influence you exert in your leadership role?

- How might ambitious staff members pursue their own careers while significantly moving the school forward towards the fulfillment of strategic objectives?
- Are your staff members attracting or repelling other ambitious educators?

School leaders must also hire based on an abundance mindset, which acts out of confidence, possibility, and faith. School leaders acknowledging the importance of the right mindset also find value in hiring talented educators. Thibodeaux advocated for hiring talented team members (Thibodeaux, 2019). For example, "...having people who can outshine you also makes it easy for you to keep learning." Onboarding ambitious and talented professionals can spur a vibrant learning community - one in which school leaders are challenged and inspired to 'keep up with the learning' of others in the team.

Forward-looking hires also add energy to the school community. They are often the members who execute on the ideas strewn about in a meeting. The truth is, every school, grade-level team, department, and committee needs 'doers' - those who will take on the additional responsibility, lead the initiative, or mentor the student club. However, remember that it's not the race on who finds the best of the best. As long as your candidates have shown a strong culture fit, give the preference to those who have the best skill set and the most diverse experience, and not in the reverse order. That way, you will avoid employee management issues since your candidates will have already achieved the value alignment with that of your school culture.

# MAKE RECOGNITION OF OTHERS A HABIT

*"Look for excuses to celebrate others, and life will find a way to celebrate you. Make your life a prayer and be the light that touches lives far, wide, and beyond." - Pooja Ruprell*

*Matt's story*

"Thank you for recognizing me."

These words were spoken to my wife in the parking garage of the *Thurgood Marshall, Baltimore Washington International Airport.* So, here's the quick story.

My wife and I were in a hurry to get to the airport and catch our flight to Phoenix. We had quickly parked the car and made our way to the airport shuttle, pick-up location in the parking garage. Joining about 8 other travelers, we rushed to our bags and boarded the vehicle, looking for a seat on the shuttle bus.

All of us, except for my wife, that is.

Instead of walking onto the bus, she stopped and acknowledged the driver. She 'saw' him. Her words were simple and yet genuine, *"Thank you for picking us up."*

In response, the driver lit up. With appreciation and a hint of pain, he replied, *"Thank you for recognizing me."*

Wow, I shrunk about 10 sizes in my seat. How self-absorbed I had been.

It was not as if I did not appreciate our driver. I did. But in my haste, I abdicated my responsibility to acknowledge and show gratitude to a fellow human being.

I was busy, yes. And my focus was on an important task, true. But I was wrong. I missed an opportunity to acknowledge and connect with my brother, and show my gratitude and appreciation for his help.

From our shuttle driver's response to my wife thanking him, I suspect a lot of other travelers walked right on by as well. Just like me.

As school leaders, how often do we fail to acknowledge individuals in our own school communities? Late for a meeting, do we walk right by a student in the hallway? Rushing to grab a document off the printer in the teacher workroom, do we avoid eye contact with a colleague standing in the doorway of his classroom? Or on the way to lunch, how often do we put our heads down to avoid engaging in a conversation? Are we just too busy doing *'things'* to connect with *people*?

(*Author's note: I can raise these questions because I am guilty of each of them.*)

The problem is that we under-index the value of connection. We undervalue the power of gratitude. We mistakenly discount the power of feeling acknowledged.

As school leaders, you should remember how much students, staff, and parents value your engagement. This includes any formal presentation, observation, or a meeting. More likely, however, engagement consists of an informal greeting in the hallway, small-talk while in line at lunch, or a quick check-in between classes to say, "Hello and thank you."

With this in mind, we gathered the three key thoughts to keep at the top of your mind in order to make recognition of others a habit.

## Make every trip count

You should approach every *'trip'* outside of your office as a strategic opportunity for connection and recognition. Not in a manipulative sense, but rather to foster inner gratitude and practice being present with your community. Cultivate a sense of appreciation for the incredible opportunity each *'trip'* presents — an opportunity to recognize staff members for what they do and the value they bring to the school. An opportunity to invest in students by providing a word of affirmation or encouragement. An opportunity to connect with parents and get their feedback related to a particular school program or initiative.

# *Invest in relationships, one positive interaction at a time*

A simple "good afternoon" in the hallway might make someone's day. At a minimum, it represents a deposit in a relational bank account. A 30–60 second conversation with a student between classes contributes to a genuine connection and builds authentic rapport. Too often, students only engage in meaningful conversation with school leaders when the subject matter is of a disciplinary nature. Though you cannot diminish the importance of professionalism when communicating with the students, it is essential to establish connection on the interpersonal level. You want them to see you as approachable, a role model, a listener, and a fair judge.

## *Keep the focus on people*

School leaders can quickly become consumed with tasks and pressing issues. Still, engaging with people is a high-value activity and, arguably, the most important aspect of the job. School leaders must seek opportunities to engage with community members — to *recognize* them for who they are and what they do within the community.

In the end, people want to be 'seen.' They desire and deserve recognition. Business leader Daymond John, best known for his star role on the hit television show Shark Tank, tells a powerful story of recognition in his new book Powershift: Transform Any Situation, Any Deal, and Achieve Any Outcome.

John initially made his mark in the business world as the founder of the iconic apparel line, FUBU. After being featured in a prominent magazine, legendary filmmaker Spike Lee wrote John a note of congratulations. In the note, Lee shared three powerful words: I see you. Overjoyed to be recognized by Lee, John held onto the note for years. Decades later, at a celebration party for Lee's receipt of an Academy Award, John had the opportunity to return the recognition. He simply walked up to Lee and said three powerful words: I see you. As John reflects on the exchange, Lee immediately caught the reference John was making from decades prior. It was a powerful and important moment. Two widely successful people - recognizing one another (John & Paisner, 2020).

As a school leader, you should be aware of the leadership platform you hold and the impact your even slightest behavioral change could have on the people around you. Your position creates impact at scale. Even during the busiest of days, you should follow my wife's lead. A simple "thank you" really will go a long way.

## *Continuing the Conversation*

From 1982 to 1993, the hit sitcom *Cheers*, streamed new episodes into millions of living rooms through television sets. The setting was a bar in Boston, Massachusetts, where a group of friends and neighbors would regularly meet. As is the case in so many bars, restaurants, gyms, places of worship, and civic groups across the world, the characters were attracted to the community they felt at *Cheers*. They appreciated being known.

As the theme song mentioned, life can be difficult and challenging; simply surviving from day to day and meeting our obligations can be an all-encompassing endeavor. As a result, "...sometimes you want to go where everybody knows your name...." At *Cheers*, patrons were recognized as individuals - ups, downs, virtues, warts, and all. The characters in the show valued this recognition so much they prioritized their schedules around regular visits to the bar. They *needed* to experience the connection they found while at *Cheers*.

This human experience carries fundamental application for school leaders. It reminds us of the human need for recognition, connection, and being known. Consequently, school leaders must create an environment where these human needs are met while at school.

In his book, *The Truth About Employee Engagement: A Fable About Addressing The Three Root Causes of Job Misery*, Patrick Lencioni identified anonymity as one of three reasons employees are not happy at work. According to Lencioni, "People cannot be fulfilled in their work if they are not known. All human beings need to be understood and appreciated for their unique qualities by someone in a position of authority (Lencioni, 2007, p. 221).

This places the responsibility of recognition on school leaders. You cannot delegate 'recognition' initiatives to the faculty. You must champion such initiatives personally.

The reality is, we all value recognition and approval from our supervisors. Lencioni continued, "People who see themselves as invisible, generic, or anonymous cannot love their jobs, no matter what they are doing (p. 221). In their best-selling book, *How Full Is Your Bucket,* Rath and Clifton emphasized the importance of recognition in the workplace, which unfortunately occurs far less often than it should. In fact, Rath and Clifton reported 65% of Americans received no recognition in the workplace in the previous year. Aptly summarized, "No wonder so many employees are disengaged" (p. 27). As a result, morale is often poor, including low employee commitment and a diminishing sense of belonging to the organization itself.

As a school leader, how often do you provide personalized, concrete, and measurable recognition to team members? When possible, do you make that recognition and appreciation public? Is recognition of others a well-established organizational norm at your school?

There are many methods for providing recognition. Opportunities include:

- Recognizing teachers and teaching teams at staff meetings;
- Publicly praising at school-wide assemblies;
- Leaving thoughtful and personalized handwritten notes of appreciation;
- Crafting congratulatory emails, distributed across the school community;
- Or even simply offering an affirming word in the hallway.

The point is to make recognition and appreciation a habit. Recognition and appreciation become part of the ethos of the school. And a culture of recognition will not return void.

As James suggested, "Giving people a vehicle to express appreciation for one another in a public forum raises the morale of the entire group, establishes a positive tone…and helps people feel acknowledged and valued" (James, 2018). Furthermore, Craig suggests recognition produces happy employees, and "Happy employees are on average 12 percent more productive than their less-happy counterparts" (Craig, 2017). In addition, employees who receive consistent recognition from their upper management report higher degrees of trust in that same person. And finally, employees who receive regular recognition are more likely to 'stick around'. In fact, the two most cited reasons for leaving a job are a lack of autonomy or respect (Craig, 2017).

In summary, establishing a culture of recognition produces the following results:

- increased morale;
- positive community tone;
- feeling of personal value;
- increased productivity;
- higher levels of trust;
- higher levels of employee loyalty.

What type of impact would these results have on your school community?

# HIRE FOR CULTURE FIT

*"The real competitive advantage in any business is one word only, which is "people". - Kamil Toume*

Organizations must get hiring right. Each new team member will have an impact on the culture. Hire well - and a healthy organizational culture further accelerates. Hire poorly - and a healthy culture can become ill (Smart & Street, 2008).

Leadership consultant Chris Cancialosi provided an acute caution to smaller organizations, such as schools. In referring to the critical nature of hiring culture fits, he suggested, "This is even more poignant within small companies that are scaling rapidly. Every hire can impact the culture and business trajectory..." (Forbes, 2016). In other words, the smaller the organization, the more critical hiring a culture fit becomes. Not only will the new hires exert some influence over the current environment, but it will also be more closely evaluated and analyzed by their colleagues.

School leaders must ask the challenging, yet powerful question, "Does the culture of our organization attract the type of candidates we desire to hire?" (Gill, 2013). The answer to this question is integral to achieving a thriving community. The type of culture an organization creates will determine the quality of team members it will be able to recruit and retain.

Selfless, team-centered, potential hires will not be attracted to a culture marked by personal agendas and a lack of continuity. As it turns out, the culture of an organization is the most critical factor in recruiting. This is especially true for the younger generation of hires, as a prevalent majority of professionals value the culture and nonmonetary benefits more than the size of their paycheck.

School leaders should always be mindful that the hiring process is a two-way street in which both you and the applicants are assessing potential future work together. You both are asking the same questions: Do I see myself here? Are there people *like me* in this organization? Will I be comfortable in this environment? Does this culture match my expectations?

Failing to understand the candidate's perspective reduces the chances for value alignment and clear communication of expectations of both parties involved. Moreover, as candidates are meeting their potential new team members, leaders must be sure to show and communicate the full dynamics of the culture. Otherwise, the potential hires may be misguided by the misrepresentation of the working environment. This could ultimately repel good hires from your organization.

School leaders must embrace the reality that the rules of the hiring game have changed. The landscape is different. In today's intense competition for talent, the balance of power has shifted away from employers and moved in favor of the potential hires. "In decades past, when the cards in the hiring process were largely held by employers, candidates were forced to bend to their will if they ever hoped to land that next dream job. But things are changing. Many in the talent space would argue that today, the power resides with the candidates" (Cancialosi, 2016). Consequently, companies and organizations across industries find themselves in an intense fight for talent.

In a recent Forbes article, Executive Coach and Leadership Consultant, Lizabeth Czepiel, emphasized the importance of recruiting talent with an eye towards long-term contribution (Council, 2018). "High performers want a challenge, a voice, and want to contribute to growing an organization. Attract them by communicating the value of the current role, the various hats they could wear and how they could grow over the years."

In other words, share your vision for *their* growth. Consider the following 5 questions:

1. How will potential team members grow and develop over the next year, 2 years, and 5 years?
2. How will the organization invest in them and their career development?
3. Does your organization support a professional and personal growth narrative a potential team member can attach to?

4. Are there examples of such growth currently thriving on your team?
5. Does your organization allow team members to take on various roles and responsibilities across the organization?

Certainly, you should pay considerable attention to recruiting exceptional team members that match the school culture fit. As legendary management guru Peter Drucker shared, "People decisions are the ultimate - perhaps the only - control of an organization. People determine the performance capacity of an organization. No organization can be better than the people it has" (Drucker, 2012. p. 145). As you step into the recruiting process, understand that this will be integral to your organization's success.

Investing into strategic and marketing efforts would yield ineffective unless you, first and foremost, focus on employee management and community building. Without having the right people on the team, placed in the right positions within the organization, and aligned by a shared purpose, your school's potential will be severely limited.

With this in mind, Schwantes identified three mandates leaders should follow:

- hire high potentials, not rockstars;
- hire for diversity;
- hire for integrity (Schwantes, 2018).

Hiring high potential employees is critical to the success of an organization, since they are the rising stars that have the interest and capacity to learn and grow together with your school. Not at the last step of their professional ladder yet, they are hungry to make an impact and are likely to be more coachable. These team members demonstrate certain qualities - "...resilience, initiative, entrepreneurial spirit, integrity, and being able to adapt to change and new challenges." It would be foolish to ignore such personal qualities over the few more years of experience. With no enthusiasm, experience would deem useless. Thus, it is critical that you remain mindful of the long-term impact and contribution your hires will make on your community.

Hiring for diversity is a matter of self-awareness and humility. School leaders should identify the areas where their own skill sets can be filled by others, and then hire accordingly (Knippenberg & Hoever, 2017). You are then to double-down on your areas of strength - the actions that will significantly move the organization forward and will yield results. There is a sense of liberation in this approach: the leader is not expected to be *the* expert in every function. Hiring for diversity also speaks to the importance of hiring team members with perspectives and experiences different from their own. This will ultimately lead to increased creativity and a more productive problem-solving, bridging organizational gaps further, and uniquely tackling issues facing your school. Further, school leaders who prioritize hiring a diverse staff serve their students and families well. When schools communicate diversity as a core value, yet fail to embody that core value in the composition of teachers in the classrooms, for example, a disconnect forms. As a result, the entire community misses an opportunity to truly enjoy the extraordinary contributions made possible through a diverse staff.

Finally, hiring for integrity increases the level of trust within a team and allows creative energies to be focused on the collaborative work. Here, "Colleagues see each other as dependable and accountable for their actions in a culture of integrity" (Schwantes, 2018). Not only will you be better off as an organization by focusing on integrity, but the environment will continue to attract team members who will preserve the school culture fit.

Indeed, the success of a school hinges on the quality of the staff. In his book, *Like A Virgin: Secrets They Won't Teach You at Business School*, entrepreneur Richard Branson emphasized this truth. "Let's get right to the point: good people are not just crucial to a business, they are the business! Finding them, managing them, inspiring them and then holding on to them is one of the most important challenges a business leader faces…" (Branson, 2013, p. 14). If you expect to rise to Branson's challenge, you will have to ensure your school culture is attractive to the most talented of applicants. When healthy school cultures are combined with top talent, there are no limits to what a school can achieve.

# CULTIVATE A SELFLESS TEAM CULTURE

*"Teamwork makes the game a little easier for each player. Teamwork implies unselfishness and unselfishness creates an environment where we execute OUR best option not MY best option."*
*- Kevin Eastman, via Twitter, February 3, 2020*

What makes the difference between a team with a strong bond as opposed to a team that never seemed to fully gel together? Why do some teams achieve above their talent level, while others languish far below their potential? And perhaps most profound, why were some teams just so much fun to be a part of, while others drained the collective energy of the group?

As complex as it is, a great deal of this variance can be attributed to culture. In particular, the degree to which team members are focused on their own achievement as opposed to the success of the collective. Selfishness is the quality to be cautious of since it may not only decrease one person's productivity, but impact performance and dynamics of the entire team.

The distinction between *selfish* culture versus *selfless* culture makes a fundamental difference at the scale of an entire organization. And the degree to which the members of an organization behave selflessly or selfishly is largely a result of the organization's prevailing culture. Strong cultures, grounded in an others-centered approach, produce selfless behavior. Conversely, "In a weak culture, we veer away from doing 'the right thing' in favor of doing 'the thing that's right for me'" (Sinek, 2014, p. 162). Leaders must be on guard. They must fight for their culture every day. When a selfless culture defines a team, incredible outcomes are possible. Not to mention that cultivating this environment will also be more engaging and interactive for school stakeholders to experience.

Duke University Men's Basketball coach, Mike Krzyzewski, perhaps best summarized what a selfless team culture looks like.

171

He described the beauty of the team concept as displayed on a basketball court where all five teammates act as one. Here, five individuals are connected and in harmony. Individual desires and preferences have been supplanted by the team's purpose. It turns out, teamwork is a prerequisite for a selfless culture. With this in mind, let's explore 3 traits of a selfless team culture.

*In a selfless team culture, credit is freely given to others.*

When a selfless culture is present, credit is given away freely. Similar to a game of *hot potato*, no one wants to be left holding the credit. Individuals recognize the interdependence of the team and the roles and responsibilities of each team member. There is a socially-approved standard that everyone must do their job well. And no one wants to let the team down.

In addition, selfless team members experience a huge amount of joy from celebrating others and giving them recognition. They identify their own success in direct proportion to the success of their colleagues. Working together and focusing on each other's strengths leads any team, in any organization, to success.

*In a selfless team culture, team members volunteer to 'step in the gap' when needed without keeping score.*

Selfless cultures are defined by mission and gratitude. In schools, such a culture manifests when team members embrace the opportunity to fill in for an absent colleague, cover a class, or meet with a student after school to prepare for an upcoming assessment. They do so out of abundance, not obligation - bringing enthusiasm to the activity for all the parties involved.

Opportunities to 'step in the gap' are not recorded on a scorecard. Rather, such acts simply support the collective mission of the team. The driving force behind this selfless service is the mission (the 'why') and gratitude (an appreciation for the opportunity to make a positive impact). Not coincidentally, the actions and the driving force behind them are each defined by a selfless approach. As a leader, you should serve as an example of selfless work, offering your hand of support to any member of the community. Finally, remember to show signs of validation and appreciation once your employees or students take actions in the name of the collective good. Truly, *what gets celebrated, gets repeated.*

*In a selfless team culture, family and personal time are valued and protected.*

Selfless cultures are not achieved organically and rarely do they occur by accident. Recruiting excellent, high-potential team members, who embody "culture fit" is only the first step. You should then embrace your employees and promote a selfless environment daily. The results are phenomenal- credit is given away to others and team members embrace the extra work necessary to operate an outstanding organization. However, leaders should take caution to ensure work does not crowd out personal space. As a school leader, you must institutionally protect the personal and family time of your team members.

Without these guardrails, a 'giving' culture will bankrupt the emotional accounts of its team members, profoundly striking the most selfless members. They will give to the point of personal imbalance. Indeed, the most dedicated faculty and staff in schools are often giving at the expense of their own wellness and that of their families. So, if a selfless culture is to last - if it is to be sustainable - you must safeguard your employees' family and personal time.

Selfless team cultures are truly transformative, but they require a lot of work and commitment (Alder-Collins, 2013). Leaders must constantly inspire their team members to move beyond their own self-interest and shift their aspiration to the well-being of others. In President John F. Kennedy's 1961 inaugural address, the new president famously appealed to the selflessness of citizens across the nation. "And so, my fellow Americans: ask not what your country can do for you - ask what you can do for your country" (JFK Library). Kennedy understood the natural inclination for humans is of a self-serving nature. He was also convinced that if the nation was to prosper in the new decade, a selfless spirit and allegiance to the country over self would be required. As a school leader, the investment you make into developing a selfless culture will be worthwhile, and the return, nearly immeasurable. And yet it must be done in a deliberate, thoughtful, and sustainable manner.

# PROMOTE FROM WITHIN TO MAKE A SUSTAINABLE ORGANIZATION

*"A leader who produces other leaders multiplies their influences."*
*- John Maxwell*

Sustainable organizations are facing both external and internal talent management issues. There is always a need to optimize the processes of talent acquisition and retention. A systematic approach to hiring that embodies your school's purpose will ensure the right hires and avoid employee pitfalls in the future.

Competition for talent is fierce. In 2000, the US Department of Education estimated that 60% of all new jobs in the 21st century will require skills that only 20% of the workforce possess (Njiraine, 2019). Further, colleges in the United States will graduate only 198,000 students to fill the shoes of 2 million baby boomers scheduled to retire between 1998 and 2018 (Deloitte Report, 2018). Add in the warp speed of innovation and creative destruction across industries, and the job market proves an unsettling terrain for job seekers and employers.

One strategy to bring order to the process for both employees and employers is to create a culture of internal promotion. Camerold Herold proposed that a staple of healthy and prospering companies is the prevalence of internal promotion. In these companies, employees enjoy clarity of expectation and have a vibrant understanding of the leader's vision. Consequently, leaders are able to distribute leadership with confidence, thereby providing a meaningful platform for employees to gain experience and grow (Herold, 2017).

As we discussed in a previous section, today's school leaders find themselves in fierce competition for top talent (Macan, 2009). In many ways, candidates enjoy higher degrees of leverage in the hiring process than ever before. The good news is, through an intentional effort to grow talent and promote from within, schools can increase employee loyalty and engagement, while developing a pipeline of internal leaders.

In a 2019 *Entrepreneur* article, Techincon Co-founder and Microsoft Senior Consultant, Rashan Dixon, urged managers to identify the high-potential leaders within their own organizations. Once identified, leaders should then intentionally develop the leadership skills of these talented individuals. According to Dixon, "When seeking new managers and leaders for your company, promoting from within may prove more effective than hiring an external candidate." He outlined the following advantages to the internal promotion model:

*Internal candidates require less time to get up to speed.* They have relational capital across the organization. They also have a familiarity with the internal operations of the organization and will thus be able to apply their energy and attention to learning the new role, as opposed to the organization itself.

*Promoting from within encourages other employees by demonstrating upward mobility within the organization is readily available.* When you promote a colleague to a senior-level role, you confirm to other team members that their efforts will be rewarded in the same way. These positive emotional associations strengthen employee commitment to the organization.

*Hiring internal candidates facilitates succession planning.* As your new hires are taking on the responsibilities of current employees, the latter are able to continue growing and focus their efforts on learning their new role. You should mentor internal leaders and help them learn about perspectives and context they otherwise wouldn't get until several years into a leadership role.

So, what traits do high-potential leaders model? Who should current leaders and managers be investing in and preparing for promotion? Dixon suggested special attention for potential investment should be given to the team members who:

- take initiative;
- demonstrate humility;
- communicate effectively;
- are excellent listeners (Dixon, 2019).

Notably, identifying these traits is relatively simple and does not require extensive data analysis and employment of complex tools and algorithms. Identifying these traits does require intentionality on the part of the executive team to establish a culture of internal staff investment and promotion. As high-potential staff recognize learning and development opportunities provided by their own school, they will be motivated to improve and learn, while increasing their organizational commitment.

School leaders must remember that retaining talent is not a passive objective. Instead, it requires awareness and active presence on the part of school leaders. MyCorporation.com CEO, Deborah Sweeney, outlined three key steps leaders can take to retain talent.

First, *create growth pathways for team members within the organization*. Do not typecast team members into specific functions, or even departments. Rather, allow their talents and skill sets to determine the specific functions they will serve. As these talents and skill sets evolve, so too their roles and assignments within the organization. That way, your employees will not be limited in their capabilities and will creatively broaden their functions and the impact they exert on the school community. Under the culture of growth, these team members will effectively tackle school issues, engage others in a similarly productive thought process, and promote proactive behavior throughout the organization.

Second, *provide talented team members with a challenging workload*. High-achievers want to be engaged and experience the tension of growth. As Sweeney recommends, "Encourage talent to take initiative, too. If they notice something in their department that the company is not doing or should be doing, allow them to pitch their plan to you for what's missing and how they plan to solve the problem." Allow them to add value where their abilities align and challenge them to go one step further.

Finally, Sweeney *encouraged leaders to make praise a regular habit*. Affirmation is powerful, and high-achievers, who take risks and step out of their comfort zones on a regular occasion, need to be encouraged. You should provide encouragement on an individual level, while also praising the team member on a corporate level as well (Sweeney, 2019). Remember, that recognition should be unique to each case and should be earned. In that way, your encouragement will be not only valued, but will also serve as motivation to improve.

Internal promotion for key roles also boosts morale. School leaders send an empowering message to their staff when current teachers and staff are provided the opportunity to accept new roles within the school. The message is '*we see the great work you are doing and recognize the value you add to our team.*'

Promoting from within also sends an affirming message to stakeholders across the school community. Such decisions speak to the talent level of the current staff members. Further, "Promoting from within also shows how the company is growing and leveraging that growth into opportunity for its current employees. It's an act of faith that gives everyone a greater sense of stability both financially and emotionally" (Foroughi, 2016). As schools face new challenges, staff members can always be confident in the knowledge, skills, and talent of their colleagues.

# LEAD WITH OPEN EYES AND FULL HEARTS

*"A good head and a good heart are always a formidable combination."*
*- Nelson Mandela*

Eyes and hearts. Analytics and emotions. The duality allows leaders to engage the head and the heart - and thereby, lead with strength and compassion. Leading across both domains will result in a much stronger value alignment and improvement in working efficiencies across all levels.

School leaders must have *open eyes* to recognize where improvements within the school community are needed. *Open eyes* allow for honest self-assessment, thereby viewing current realities as they really are.

At the same time, *full hearts* allow school leaders to keep *people* - students, families, and staff - at the forefront at all times. Questions such as, '*How will this change or decision impact people?*' become the lens through which school leaders operate.

Leadership intelligence arises when one can manage one's own and others' emotions effectively (emotional intelligence), when one experiences a deeper desire and willingness to see the meaning of what one is doing (spiritual intelligence), and when one possesses advanced logical and analytical skills (rational intelligence). Spiritual intelligence belongs to the existential query field and answers the question "Why?" A leader should possess all three intelligences and should be able to maintain them in an integrative good balance.

So, let's explore what it means to lead with open eyes and full hearts.

*Recognize reality and lead your team through it*. School leaders must resist the temptation to paint an 'all-is-well' picture if that is not reality. Instead, they should present a clear assessment of the challenges facing the school and then lead staff *through* present reality to a brighter future. Leadership expert Jim Collins dedicated an entire chapter of his bestselling book, *Good to Great: Why Some Companies Make the Leap...and Others Don't*, to the concept of *confronting the brutal facts*. As Collins states, "It is impossible to make good decisions without infusing the entire process with an honest confrontation of the brutal facts" (p. 88). As schools start to value the brutal truth, they begin to clearly see the areas that need improvement and can initiate the process of transformation.

*Conduct honest self-assessment as it relates your own strengths.* It is critical school leaders recognize their own strengths and weaknesses. They must then relentlessly dedicate their time and efforts to continuous improvement. In his leadership best-seller, *The 21 Irrefutable Laws of Leadership*, John Maxwell writes, "What you get is not determined by what you want. It's determined by who you are" (Maxwell, 2008, p. 90). The most direct path to school improvement is *leadership development*. School leaders will attract team members who share their values and approach to education. Industrious, virtuous, and talented educators will be attracted to school leaders who also possess these same traits. Conversely, the inverse also holds true.

*Objectively Assess Your Team.* School leaders must form an objective and honest assessment of each team member. To do so, consider the following 7 questions:

1. Are people assigned to the right jobs/roles?
2. Are team members playing to their strengths?
3. How does each team member propel the school towards its strategic objectives?
4. Does each team member embody the school's core values?
5. What areas of development are needed for each team member?
6. As a leader, are you providing the appropriate support?
7. Are you providing room for the individual to grow?

## Assume best intentions.

I (Marc) generally carry with me a coin in my pocket. It reminds of the frailties of life and how I am here today but possibly gone tomorrow, that I owe my students everything I can offer. I got the idea from Ryan Holiday and am grateful to him for enlightening me (and many others) on the wisdom of stoicism.

On a recent Friday, I was scheduled to speak to a special group of formerly incarcerated prisoners on how to develop better habits and time management as part of Georgetown University's Pivot Program. In my rush to arrive early, I had forgotten my coin. During my lesson, I briefly mentioned my forgotten coin in passing to the audience. At the end of the talk, a former prisoner approached me and in a closed hand, concealing something, approached me to shake my hand. My immediate thought was that he was going to pass me something illicit or some form of contraband.

Instead, it was a coin, quite possibly the only coin he had. My initial thought was shame, how could I possibly assume the worse? But soon my thoughts were flooded with another emotion. Gratefulness. I was grateful for his kindness. I was grateful for his thoughtfulness, but I was most grateful for the valuable lesson he taught me - do not assume the worst of people. Instead, assume the best.

As he handed me the coin he said, "so you will never forget your coin again."

He is right, I won't.

Operating from a position of best intent requires self-assuredness and communicates strength. It also creates room for abundance and allows grace to inform interactions. In an article entitled, *3 Benefits In My Life From Assuming Positive Intent*, Tom Blair identified three positive results from assuming best intent in others - *better communication; accelerated personal growth; and increased interpersonal trust* (Blair, 2018). When best intent is the framework from which a leader operates, good things are 'allowed to happen.' Conversely, paranoia, lack of trust, and cynicism become obstacles that prevent your employees from doing their best work, while also negatively impacting your school's value alignment and collaborative environment.

## Commit to empathy

See your staff as people first, professionals second. This does not suggest leaders should be entrenched in the personal lives of their team members. It does, however, suggest effective leaders approach professionals through a people lens. According to emotional intelligence expert Harvey Deutschendorf, empathy is the most critical leadership skill in today's workplace. Strong cultures of empathy produce collaborative, happy, creative, loyal, and engaged staff (Deutschendorf, 2008). Empathetic school leaders connect with their teams. They bring team members into a place of belonging, contribution, and engagement.

## Serve without expectation of return

School leaders operate from a 'full heart' by acting as servant leaders. In this way, they serve others as an outflow of a grateful and contented heart. They are not seeking something in return; there is no manipulation at play. Instead, servant leaders place incredible value on people and enjoy investing in them. It turns out, selfless leadership empowers team members and also strengthens the position of the leader by making them more likable and credible. "Simply put, people serve people, not companies. That's the key to the undervalued leadership component of likeability: a genuine servant mentality" (Hayzlett, 2015).

Leading with 'open eyes and full hearts' creates a powerful synergy. The most effective school leaders recognize the power of "and" - leading with objectivity "and" emotional sensitivity. Head and heart - they lead their school communities from a position of true strength.

# MAKE STRATEGIC PLANNING A HABIT

*"A vision without a strategy remains an illusion." - Lee Bolman*

Effective vision and mission statements facilitate the strategic planning process. As school leaders craft annual, 3-year, and 5-year strategic objectives, alignment with vision and mission is critical. If a school establishes strategic objectives which do not support their overarching standards and goals, the achievement of these objectives can subsequently derail the school and limit its effectiveness.

As a result, strategic planning should be completed with an eye towards the school's vision and mission statements. When this occurs, schools establish a culture of alignment and consistent progress towards their 'why'. Staff are able to connect with the organizational objectives established to the school's past and present.

A culture of alignment is an orderly culture, where employees understand the goals of the organization, embrace clearly established expectations for their own performance, have the resources needed to succeed, and enjoy open communication. In an aligned culture, team members understand how their work supports the bigger picture, while enjoying the confidence that results achieved will endure well into the future. The following questions will provide some guidance as you start to engage in the strategic planning process.

21 Strategic Planning Questions for School Leaders:

1. Have you communicated the key strategic objectives you have established for the upcoming school year?
2. How will you continually communicate the strategic objectives throughout the school year?

3. Has the WHY of each objective been effectively communicated?
4. Have you painted a crystal clear picture, in your own mind, of what success will look like for each objective?
5. Have you identified a connection between the upcoming year's strategic objectives and your school's mission and vision?
6. Are you and your staff emotionally connected with the objectives established for the upcoming school year?
7. Does your staff possess the skills needed to accomplish the objectives?
8. If a skills gap exists, how will you provide the appropriate training in a timely manner?
9. Are staff assigned to the correct roles in order to best support achieving the strategic objectives?
10. Have you studied the upcoming year's school calendar to identify time periods where staff may have particularly burdensome demands placed on their time?
11. Have you identified leaders across the staff to serve as sub-committee chairs, liaisons, and representatives throughout the school year?
12. Are adequate resources allocated to support the work your team will engage in?
13. Where do you predict additional resources may be needed later in the school year?
14. How will progress towards the goals be measured?
15. How often will progress towards achieving the strategic objectives be measured?
16. How will progress towards achieving the strategic objectives be communicated across all the levels of your organization?
17. How will progress towards achieving the strategic objectives be celebrated?
18. Are you and your team prepared to pivot if sufficient progress is not taking place?

19. How will you determine when a pivot may be necessary?
20. Are you prepared to face resentment, questioning, and criticism throughout the school year?
21. How will you keep your WHY in the forefront of your mind throughout the year?

# COMMIT TO ENSURING EQUITY FOR ALL COMMUNITY MEMBERS

*"Learning can only happen in spaces where armor is neither necessary nor rewarded." – Brenee Brown, May 7, 2019, Twitter*

Of all the responsibilities that a school leader may be accountable for, perhaps none is more important than providing a safe, inclusive, and equitable environment for students and staff. As we all know, the world is a difficult place, full of evil, inequality, and bias. We also recognize that life is not easy. It can be downright hard.

I once saw a wonderful statement on the marquee of an elementary school in Tennessee. The statement went something like this: "Everyone is carrying a heavy load on their journey; don't make their burden even heavier." I loved this acknowledgement - despite our sometimes tough bravado or emotionally closed-off projection, all of us have burdens to bear. We all hurt. We all endure pain.

Schools must not add to that burden - not for students or staff. Taking this responsibility a step further, schools should nourish the environment where everyone feels respected, safe, and valued. To accomplish this, school leaders must thoughtfully engage in many facets of school life.

First, students should see themselves represented in their school experience. A diverse staff is critical. When students do not see themselves represented in the front of the classroom, it sends a less than inclusive message to them. School leaders should also make sure that students see themselves and their experiences in the content they engage with. For example, female students should read stories where female characters assume strong leadership roles.

Another critical aspect to equity is voice. Teachers must ensure all students are comfortable, safe, and are encouraged to share their viewpoints and experiences, all within a respectful dialogue. When this is not part of the culture, societal inequities are brought into the classroom, factions are reinforced, and unity is hindered. Work together with school experts on finding what standards your staff is committed to upholding within your community. Educating your staff members on how to lead the classroom and supporting the learning of soft skills is integral to ensuring that the entire school upholds community expectations around diversity, equity, and inclusion. Starting from the youngest of your stakeholders, school leaders must provide education on the importance of diversity, equity and inclusion so that students begin to find their voice as young people who will become engaged, responsible, and respectful citizens.

Another critical equity component for schools is socioeconomic. Particularly acute in highly-affluent regions, school leaders must be intentional to avoid institutional reminders of those who 'have' and those who 'do not have.' Our schools must be places of refuge and belonging. When socio-economic disparities are reinforced - through policy, bias, or structure - community is undermined, school culture erodes, and most acutely, children are hurt.

HuffPost contributor Paul Schmitz, thoughtfully addressed the issue of equity in non-profit organizations. As he points out, many organizations identify equity and inclusion as pillars or even core values. Nonetheless, the composition of senior leadership and those making decisions regarding equity are often not diverse themselves. This is problematic, because they can't truly understand the problems and do not recognize the inequities that cause disruption within the community. Such blind spots often lead to ineffective or even misguided policies. Simply put, there is a lack of empathy.

As Schmitz suggests, "We need a breadth of people and perspective at our tables to properly diagnose problems, interpret data, choose strategies, consider trade-offs and unintended consequences, define success, and evaluate whether we are succeeding" (Schmitz, 2018). Without a diverse group of people at the proverbial table, organizations cannot make decisions through an equity lens. Indeed, for all voices to be heard, all voices must be represented.

Moving from problem identification to taking action, Schmidt outlined three key steps towards building a more equitable organization.

- First, *"Be aware - even vigilant - about who is and is not at the table."* If we are to solve problems or create school policies which produce equity for stakeholders, those in policy-making positions must first identify the perspectives and experiences represented in the room, and those which are not.

- Second, *"Examine our breadth of perspectives."* Reflecting upon the degree to which the leadership team's shared experiences represent those of the organization as a whole, is a critical step to unearthing systemic equity issues within the organization. Only then, can leaders recognize potential blind spots and implicit biases to address.

- Finally, *"Commit - internally and even publicly - to goals for increasing the diversity of people at our table to better represent our community or population we are working to impact."* This final step creates accountability, both within the leadership team, and across the school community. Once a commitment to equity is made, an expectation of action is established (Schmitz, 2016).

School leaders must understand that equity is not a naturally occurring phenomenon. Left unattended, inequity will persist and grow. If schools are to be a place where every student and every staff member are equally valued as community members - recognized for the specific talents and abilities they contribute to the school - strategic and intentional efforts must be taken.

In short, schools should be places where every community member is free to invest their whole-self into learning and growing. Schools should be places where all community members enjoy voice and agency. A place where every community member is valued, appreciated, and loved for the unique and precious human being they are. And that is a worthy pursuit.

# EMPLOY A SHARED LEADERSHIP MODEL

*"...when a leader has the humility to distribute power across the*
*organization, the strength of the company becomes less dependent*
*on one person and is thus better able to survive"*
*(Simon Sinek, p. 211, Leaders Eat Last).*

Over the last 15 years, technology has ushered in an era of extraordinary transformation, transforming nearly every aspect of our lives. Facebook, Twitter, YouTube, and Instagram are now vital components of our daily lives. At the time of this writing, LinkedIn is closing in on 600 million users. Netflix has revolutionized our viewing habits. 5G technology has arrived. Personal banking is done from our mobile devices, while groceries are purchased from the couch and delivered to our door. Increasingly, consumers demand usability, convenience, and world-class customer service.

Indeed, the pace of change is as dizzying as it is ubiquitous. Consequently, organizations must be responsive to this high-demand environment. That responsiveness must be grounded in adaptability and the capacity to efficiently change processes, products, and services. In many ways, the leverage has shifted to the consumer - and to thrive, organizations must deliver their product or service more efficiently, innovatively, and compassionately than ever before.

The reality facing schools and school leaders is no exception. As a result, you should consider several questions:

- What type of leadership framework best allows schools to effectively engage with change?
- How can school leaders create a culture welcoming of innovation - within their classrooms, across their school leaders teams, and within their boards?

- What type of leadership style facilitates the organizational resilience needed in order to successfully face the unique challenges facing schools in the change era?

In response to these questions, a *shared leadership* model provides the greatest opportunities for schools to succeed in today's demanding environment. *Shared leadership* is not new to literature. Referred to by many names, including *distributed leadership, democratic leadership*, the *flat organization*, and *empowered leadership*, this approach to leadership is grounded in the idea that successful leaders do not hoard influence for themselves or only for those with a specific title of corner office.

Instead, *shared leadership* provides staff, throughout the school community, with the authority and influence needed to make decisions which extend beyond their specific title or role within the organization. It operates from a belief that decisions are best made by the people most intimately engaged with the problem itself. Foundationally, well-informed decisions are crucial to the success of any organization in the era of change. If schools are to thrive, decision-making authority cannot be reserved for senior leadership, but rather should be equally distributed throughout the organization.

According to Ancona and Backman, change is often best implemented from the bottom of the traditional, organizational pyramid. Citing Southwest Airlines as an example, "…front-line employees took the lead in devising new ways to reduce turnaround times and developing electronic ticketing." *Shared leadership* communicates to the entire team that expertise exists throughout the organization. And where expertise exists, the authority to make decisions is granted. Organizations such as Southwest Airlines also work to "…inject more lateral and external voices into the generation, vetting, and selection of ideas." The idea reinforced here is a commitment to obtaining the most representative information and placing influence in the hands of those with that information (Ancona & Backman, 2010).

The era of change further requires schools to possess wide-ranging competencies. New challenges arise constantly, and in response, a broad cadre of leaders and decision-makers are needed. Someone in the school has the knowledge, experience, and skills to take a leading role in solving *any* problem. But no one person, or small echo chamber of people, has the knowledge, experience, and skills to solve *all* problems.

School leaders must create a culture where ideas are valued and people feel safe so that they will share their ideas without fear of rejection. As leadership expert Kevin Eastman suggested, "For a team or organization trying to stay ahead of the game, no idea is silly. What is silly –or worse—is not offering an idea that just might turn out to be the one that makes the difference. Put it out there!" (Eastman, 2019). A team approach to idea generation is truly needed. As a school leader, once you start to cultivate such a vision, your staff will begin to value each other more and the collaborative environment will thrive.

In addition, Carsten Tams encouraged organizations in the change era to adopt a shared leadership model. "The shared leadership model conceptualizes leadership as a set of shared practices that can and should be enacted by people at all levels. Leadership is understood as a dynamic and multi-directional group process rather than a role exercised by a select few at the top." Tams continued to describe how a shared leadership model, marked by a "collective construction process," creates a more facilitative environment for innovation and change management (Tams, 2018). The shared leadership model also propels organizations towards their maximum effectiveness and power. Sinek suggested organizations actually increase their collective power as they transfer decision-making authority from the executive ranks and to the front lines (Sinek, 2014). "The more energy is transferred from the top of the organization to those who are actually doing the job, those who know more about what's going on on a daily basis, the more powerful the organization and the more powerful the leader" (p. 184).

The dynamism created by a shared leadership framework stands in stark contrast to the top-down, bureaucratic machinations of the traditional hierarchy. Indeed, *flat* organizations are able to efficiently respond, pivot, and even change the course of actions. Schools should strategically move in this direction, catalyzing and engaging staff, while ushering the best ideas to the table. Absent the best information, school leaders cannot expect to make the best possible decisions.

Schools that operate from a shared leadership framework also enjoy greater organizational speed. As Craig (2018) described, "...flat organization cuts through some of the clutter. Responsibility and project-ownership get localized within your teams, and those teams in turn have greater autonomy..." Craig further suggested "...flat leadership structures allow decisions to be made in places where those decisions have the greatest consequence." Again, decisions are made by those closest to the situation and who most intimately live with the subsequent results on a daily basis. The quality of those decisions are likely to be greater and the time required of the school to move to action is decreased.

Increasingly, top-down leadership structures are coming under scrutiny. Wagner used the terms "broken" and "relic" to describe the top-down models still utilized by many organizations (Wagner, 2012, p. 229). He strongly encouraged organizations to embrace a *democratized* leadership model, where the ideas of all team members are upholded. The change era no longer allows for bureaucratic leadership. It requires those closest to the action, who have the best information, make empowered and timely decisions. This means they must have the authority to respond and to act and they must be celebrated when they do. You should review systems, procedures, and norms across your school to identify, and subsequently eliminate, any structural inefficiencies to a shared leadership model.

As a school leader, it is critical that you recognize the constant change and creative disruption of the status quo is prevalent in the workplace. From innovations in online and blended learning, to the considerable social stresses facing our students, change is constant. This makes necessary an innovative approach to school governance. Said succinctly, schools must be nimble if they are to thrive in a fast-moving world. A shared leadership model makes this possible.

Achieving a shared leadership governance structure for your school can be challenging. It may require a paradigm shift in thinking. Perhaps most important, moving towards a flat leadership culture may feel threatening to those in positions of senior leadership. And yet shared leadership is not a threat at all. A democratized leadership model does not eliminate the need for Department Chairs, Division Heads, Assistant Heads of School, or Heads of School. It simply expands their resources for effective decision-making by bringing the best information to the table. Better information results in better decisions. And better decisions result in more effective leadership.

Consider the following reflection questions as you work towards a *shared leadership* model in your school:

- Does your school, division, department, or grade-level formally engage all stakeholders in decision-making and strategic planning?
- Are there specific team members who have not been appropriately engaged and/or empowered?
- How are you preparing your team members for increasing responsibility and decision-making authority?
- Are you aligning your school's strategic plan to a shared leadership framework?
- How will your hiring practices be impacted as you fully implement a shared leadership approach?
- What skills will new team members need to possess?

# EMBRACE CHANGE

*"Change is the law of life. And those who look only to the past or present are certain to miss the future." - John F. Kennedy*

In the previous discussion related to *shared leadership*, we introduced the prevalence of change in today's leadership environment and examined the type of leadership structure schools should implement. We now take our discussion of change a step further by emphasizing the need for school leaders to not only accept change, but *embrace* it. Many organizations, and people for that matter, are reluctant to embrace change. Some consider preparing for change as a waste of time, money and effort. They remain unconvinced as to the positive impacts of change, and thus reservedly approach the subject (Bowe, 2011). These organizations fail to realize the potential for growth through change. They also fail to identify the potential for achieving organizational success when the change is aligned with the organization's goals and objectives.

Truly, change impacts all of us. It has no respect for position or industry. In fact, people and organizations are constantly engaging with change - either entering into a *change event*, presently experiencing a *change event*, or just emerging from a *change event*. From our personal lives to our family lives, change is ever present.

As a result, effective school leaders embrace change. They lean into it and attack the change forces they are experiencing. In doing so, leaders exert their personal and organizational resources to positively impact the change and make the best of the situation. Sturt and Nordstrom (2016) instructed leaders to remember 4 key actions in the face of change:

1. ***Further democratize information.***
Your team's level of anxiety and uncertainty determines your measure of response. The more acute the change, the more

critical an open-information sharing approach is. In the absence of information, people assume the worst. As a leader, you must step into that space with transparency and accurate information.

2.  *Take a step back and develop a thoughtful plan of action.*
As a leader, you must separate yourself from the emotion attached to the issue at hand. Then, break your school's plan of action down into small, measurable actions. Avoid the temptation to solve the problem in a single action. Such heroic actions rarely result in optimal results. Instead, simply lead your team to take the *next best step.*

3.  *Proactively respond to conflicts.*
In times of change, leadership teamwork is essential. To successfully meet the challenges associated with the change event your school is experiencing, full engagement and collaboration of all team members is a must. Everyone's gifts and experience will be needed.

4.  *Commit to encouragement.*
In times of change, team members will take their emotional cues from the leader. Calm, positive, and measured leaders will engender a similarly constructive response from their team and facilitate a successful outcome. Frantic, negative, and reactionary leaders will engender the opposite (Sturt and Nordstrom, 2016). Be aware of these consequences as you develop your own leadership style.

In his 2011 book, *Change Leader: Learning To Do What Matters Most*, Michael Fullan outlined seven principles for effective change leadership. School leaders will likely identify with many of the leadership principles herein. These seven change leadership principles mentioned below will serve as guideposts in creating a school culture that embraces change - even harnessing it for growth and innovation.

*Effective change leaders engage in the work as learners.* There is no substitute for rolling up your sleeves and doing the work, shoulder to shoulder with your team. In the classroom, the '*sage on the stage*' has been replaced by a more active and engaging instructional approach. Leadership has experienced a similar change in landscape. Today, employees respect their supervisors more when the supervisor engages in the work directly with them - offering help, not criticism.

*Effective change leaders are both mission oriented and empathic.* You should demonstrate deep conviction for the course of action the organization has established. Be determined and vigorously pursue achievement. Committed to the mission, effective change leaders challenge the status quo. At the same time, they respect and seek out the ideas of those who may disagree with them. To you, achieving success should be a *'together endeavor,'* not an individual pursuit.

*Effective change leaders recognize demonstrated effectiveness compels people to change.* Directives do not result in transformation or empowerment. At best, they provide temporary compliance. Be sure to demonstrate the conviction and patience to invest in a course of action over a long period of time. Effective change leaders know many within the organization will not truly embrace the change initiative until they see its effectiveness demonstrated. In the interim, effective change leaders remain steadfastly committed to the course of action while allowing buy-in to gradually build from within the team.

*Effective change leaders create an environment that is both competitive and collaborative.* Leading effective change requires significant organizational energy. With this in mind, effective change leaders create a team-first environment. The organization is focused on achieving shared objectives. Within that structure, an expectation of excellence and commitment allows for a competitive, yet collaborative environment to thrive. The competition is not about jockeying for internal positioning. Instead, it is based on the belief that as long as we are all pulling in the same direction, our individual successes only serve to propel the *team* forward.

*Effective change leaders embody both humility and an irrepressible confidence.* Confident leaders are comfortable enough in themselves and their ability to be humble. They do not seek credit or need affirmation for coming up with the "game winning idea." Effective change leaders are focused on achieving organizational objectives and their validation results from team success. They delight in growing the confidence and abilities of those they lead.

*Effective change leaders utilize data, while valuing wisdom.* Data is a wonderful tool. And in today's organizational environment it is omnipresent. Effective change leaders leverage any valuable data to strategically inform decision-making. At the same time, they do not overly rely on it. They apply wisdom to the analytics - common sense to the spreadsheet. Effective change leaders make decisions based on the data, while also reflecting on how decisions will impact people. As discussed previously, they lead with open eyes and full hearts.

*Effective change leaders lean into the contrast of simple and complex.* Decisions will often be both simple and complex. Why is this so? Because leading change involves leading people - and people are complex. While the objective, action step to a *people-situation may* be simple to identify, in execution it could be extraordinarily complex. Effective change leaders understand this and engage with team members adeptly.

There are simply no shortcuts to effective change leadership. When experiencing school-wide change, the best school leaders provide vision, set clear priorities, and skillfully execute on strategic initiatives. In doing so, they embrace dualities such as simplicity and complexity, data and wisdom, competition and collaboration, as well as ambition and empathy. Effective change leaders roll up their sleeves and work alongside their teams.

# SECTION 4 REFERENCE LIST

Ancona, D. and E. Backman, (2010), *Distributed leadership: going from pyramids to networks, Leadership Excellence, 27, pp. 11-12.*

Alder-Collins, J. (2013). *Courage and selflessness in professional actions: but are they enough? International Nursing Review, 60(2), 201–204. doi: 10.1111/inr.12021*

Backman, Maurie. (2019). *Why Aren't More Workers Taken Parental Leave? Fast Company. Retrieved June 8, 2019.*

Branson, R. (2012). *Like A Virgin: Secrets They Won't Teach You at Business School. New York, NY: Portfolio/Penguin.*

Blair, T. (2018, July 6). *3 Benefits In My Life From Assuming Positive Intent. Retrieved from https://medium.com/@BlairOutLoud/3-benefits-in-my-life-from-assuming-positive-intent-8c2024400d8.*

Bowe, R (2011). *Change Management Coach. Washington DC: Oxford Press.*

Burg, B. & Mann, J.D. (2007). *The Go-Giver: A Little Story About A Powerful Business Idea. New York, NY: Portfolio/Penguin.*

Burkus, D. (2020). *"Extrinsic vs. Intrinsic Motivation at Work." Psychology Today. https://www.psychologytoday.com/us/blog/creative-leadership/202004/extrinsic-vs-intrinsic-motivation-work*

Cancialosi, C. 2016. "It's Time To Redefine the Rules Of Employee Engagement." Forbes, February 1. www.forbes.com/sites/ chriscancialosi/2016/02/01/its-time-toredefine-the-rules-of-employee-engagement. Friedman, L.H.

Cancialosi, C. (2016). Why You Can't Ignore Culture In Your Recruiting Process. Forbes. Retrieved May 6, 2019.

Collins, J. C. 1., & Porras, J. I. (1994). Built to last: successful habits of visionary companies. New York, NY: Harper Business.

Council, F. (2018, July 13). Council Post: 14 Ways To Find Valuable Candidates In The War For Talent. Retrieved from https://www.forbes.com/sites/forbescoachescouncil/2018/07/13/14-ways-to-find-valuable-candidates-in-the-war-for-talent/#24a1abda6d1

Craig, W. (2017). 3 Reasons Why Employee Recognition Will Always Matter. Forbes. Retrieved February 2, 2020.

Craig, W. (2018). What Businesses Need In Order to Develop a Flat Structure of Leadership. Forbes. Retrieved March 7, 2019.

Deloitte Research, "It's 2008: Do You Know Where Your Talent Is? Why Acquisition and Retention Strategies Don't Work." Copyright © 2008 Deloitte Development LLC

Deutschendorf, H. (2008). The other kind of smart: boost your emotional intelligence for greater power and joy at home, work, and play. Edmonton, Alta.: Harmony House Press.

Dixon, R. (2019, May 24). How to Identify and Nurture the Leadership Potential of Your Employees. Retrieved from https://www.entrepreneur.com/article/333935

Drucker, P. (1990). *Managing the Non-Profit Organization: Principles and Practices*. New York, NY: HarperCollins.

*ERG Theory*. (n.d.). Encyclopedia of Management Theory. doi: 10.4135/9781452276090.n87

Foroughi, C. K., Werner, N. E., McKendrick, R., Cades, D. M., & Boehm-Davis, D. A. (2016). Individual differences in working-memory capacity and task resumption following interruptions. *Journal of Experimental Psychology: Learning, Memory, and Cognition, 42(9),* 1480–1488.

Gill, G. (2013). Culture, Complexity, and Informing: How Shared Beliefs Can Enhance Our Search for Fitness. *Informing Science: The International Journal of an Emerging Transdiscipline, 16,* 071–098. doi: 10.28945/1778

Hatfield, E., Purvis, J., & Rapson, R. L. (2016). Equity Theory of Organizations. *Global Encyclopedia of Public Administration, Public Policy, and Governance,* 1–11. doi: 10.1007/978-3-319-31816-5_90-1

Hayzlett, J. (2015). *Think Big, Act Bigger: The Rewards of Being Relentless*. Irvine, US: Entrepreneur Press.

Herold, C. (2017). *Vivid Vision: A Remarkable Tool For Aligning Your Business Around a Shared Vision of the Future.* LionCrest.

Herzberg, F. (2003). One more time: How do you motivate employees? *Harvard Business Review, 81(1),* 86.

James, V. (2018). *7 Tips for Creating a Positive Workplace Culture. www.inc.com*. Retrieved on February 14, 2019.

*JFK Library*. (n.d.). Retrieved from https://www.jfklibrary.org/

John, D., & Paisner, D. (2020). *Powershift: transform any situation, close any deal, and achieve any outcome.* New York: Currency.

Eastman, K. (2020, May 12). *Kevin Eastman (@kevineastman). Retrieved from https://twitter.com/kevineastman?ref_src=twsrc^google |twcamp^serp|twgr^author*

Knippenberg, D. V., & Hoever, I. J. (2017). *Team Diversity and Team Creativity. Oxford Scholarship Online. doi: 10.1093/oso/9780190222093.003.0003*

Landy, F. J., & Conte, J. M. (2013). *Work in the 21st century: An introduction to industrial and organizational psychology (4th ed.). John Wiley & Sons, Inc.*

Lencioni, P. (2016). *The truth about employee engagement: a fable about addressing the three root causes of job misery. San Francisco, CA: Jossey-Bass, Wiley.*

Lepper, M. R., Greene, D., & Nisbett, R. E. (1973). *Undermining children's intrinsic interest with extrinsic rewards: A test of the "overjustification" hypothesis. Journal of Personality and Social Psychology, 28, 129–137.*

Macan, T. (2009), *"The employment interview: A review of current studies and directions for future research," Human Resource Management Review, 19 (3), 203–218.*

MacDonald, L. (2000). *Evaluating and Managing Cumulative Effects: Process and Constraints. Environmental Management. 26.*

Maxwell, J. (1998). *The 21 Irrefutable Laws of Leadership: Follow Them and People Will Follow You. Nashville, TN: Thomas Nelson.*

McClelland, D. C. (1961). *The achieving society.* New York: The Free Press.

Njiraine, Dorothy. (2019). *The Influence of Internal Promotion and Training Incentives on Employee Performance at University of Nairobi. European Journal of International Management.* 11. 63-79.

Sinek, S. (2014). *Leaders Eat Last: Why Some Teams Pull Together and Others Don't.* New York, NY: Portfolio/Penguin.

Smart, G., & Street, R. (2008). *Who: the A method for hiring.* New York: Ballantine Books.

Schmitz, P., & Schmitz, P. (2018, July 19). *Applying An Equity Mirror to Collective Impact.* Retrieved from https://www.fsg.org/blog/applying-equity-mirror-collective-impact

Schwantes, M. (2018, March 27). *7 Harsh Truths That Will Improve Your Leadership Skills Overnight.* Retrieved from https://www.inc.com/marcel-schwantes/7-brutal-truths-every-smart-leader-needs-to-constantly-revisit.html

Sweeney, D. (2019). *Develop Talented Employees Using These 3 Strategies. Business2community.* Retrieved June 24, 2019.

Sturt, S. & Nordstrom, T. (2016). *6 Dos and Don'ts of Leading Through Change. Forbes.* Retrieved April 3, 2020.

re:Work. (2018). *Project Aristotle.* Retrieved from https://rework.withgoogle.com/print/guides/572131265 5835136/

Tams, C. (2018, September 10). *Bye-Bye, Heroic Leadership. Here Comes Shared Leadership.* Retrieved from https://www.forbes.com/sites/carstentams/2018/03/09/b

*ye-bye-heroic-leadership-here-comes-shared-leadership/#3382be582c67*

Thibodeaux, C. (1976) "Performance Analysis: A System for Increasing in Piano Students an Awareness of Stylistic Interpretation as Applied to Selected Twentieth Century Piano Music" PhD., diss., University of Oklahoma, pp. 175-179 and 264-269.

Ronthy, M. (2006). LQ – Ledarskapets intelligens – En nödvändighet för framtidens ledare [LQ – Leadership intelligence – A necessity for future leaders] Kristianstad, Sweden: Kristianstads Boktryckeri.

# CONCLUSION

*"The most basic of all human needs is to understand and be understood. The best way to understand people is to listen to them." - Ralph Nichols*

Achieving school culture fit begins by listening. We have provided the tools and framework to help you listen to your stakeholders to discover their jobs-to-be-done. Identifying and obtaining a deep understanding of each stakeholder's jobs-to-be-done promotes empathy. It also allows school leaders to deploy resources strategically. School leaders that understand stakeholders' jobs-to-be-done and match it to their school's purpose, achieve school culture fit.

Their schools become places where communication thrives, stakeholders are engaged and feel valued, instructional and non-instructional staff see themselves as integral contributors to the community, and a place in which the sustaining of school culture fit is promoted through a shared trust.

Obtaining school culture fit is a process. The process begins with discovery. It then moves to identifying stakeholders and exploring how to best support them, while delivering exceptional outcomes in support of your school's jobs-to-be-done. The process of obtaining school culture fit is never finished. In fact, school culture fit must be constantly nourished and tended to, much like a garden. Thus, school leaders are equipped with the flywheel for continuous evaluation. These inputs, successfully addressed, will keep the momentum going. And finally, school leaders must also ensure they are modeling and holding others accountable in living out the traits all schools must embody to ensure school culture fit is sustainable.

This book is a framework and a tool for ongoing reflection and discussion at your school. Some of the specific applications will look slightly different for individual schools and situations. The principles, however, are highly applicable to every school. We challenge you to thoughtfully and enthusiastically embark on this discovery journey as you seek school culture fit for your school community.

Made in the USA
Middletown, DE
29 January 2021